Waiting for a Miracle

for a Miracle

An Account of Love

To Rose Greene
From Lewis & Latasha
Enjoy!
And Kimberly

Eleanor Hinton
5-3-97

Eleanor Hinton

Library of Congress Card Catalog Number: 96-94221

ISBN 1-57502-239-7

Cover artwork by K.P.

Printed in the USA by

MORRIS
PUBLISHING

3212 E. Hwy 30
Kearney, NE 68847
800-650-7888

Dedication

This book is dedicated to K.P., all children like K.P., and to those individuals who are providing care for a loved one with any type of disability.

I also dedicate this book to my devoted sons, Jimmy and Jerry, who always found time to give loving attention and constant support to K.P. and me.

I further dedicate this book to the staff at the National Children's Center of Washington, D.C., who gave many years of training and loving care to K.P.

Finally, this book is dedicated to K.P.'s present caregivers: MedSource Community Services, Vocational Services, Inc. (VSI), and the Prince George's County Department of Family Services (Individuals with Disabilities Division), all of Maryland.

Acknowledgements

I would like to acknowledge, with a distinct sense of gratitude, Freda Barton-Haleem, whose expertise, talents and friendship played a major role in encouraging me to write this book.

I am also indebted to Elder Charles Pender for his advice, encouragement and spiritual guidance in making this book possible.

A special thanks to my typist, Betty Prosise, for her patience and untiring efforts to type and retype the manuscript. A thank you also to Pamela Page for proofreading and preparing the final draft.

My heartfelt thanks to Jeff Faulkner, who edited this book for print.

I also wish to express sincere appreciation to all other persons who shared information and helped me in so many ways.

Table of Contents

Introduction

This book tells the story of our family's love and commitment to keeping K.P., my mentally disabled son, at home with his family. This first-hand account reveals the love and bonding between a mentally disabled child and his mother. I am sharing my experience so that other families with disabled loved ones to care for will know that there is someone else who bears this responsibility, too. I hope this book will help others to understand the need to be strong and press on as advocates for their loved ones.

For fifteen years or more, I have watched my son exhibit episodes of violent outbursts while on different medications. It seemed very apparent that these medications only increased the number of episodes. Modern-day medicine has failed my son. Today, we have been blessed with the technology that provides us with the opportunity to explore many new approaches to healing, bringing about "wholeness" in our being. A more holistic approach to healing, such as herbal, spiritual, or any other alternative approach, could be considered as well.

I am writing this story in the simplest way, hoping that anyone who has knowledge of such treatments or alternatives will contact me. I also hope that everyone reading this book will be able to understand the frustration and struggle my family has experienced.

I have written what might be called a case study. The psychologicals, medical records, individualized educational plans and other records accompanying the text will help to tell the story in more detail. It is my wish that this book will motivate and give inspiration to those involved in a similar struggle. It is also my prayer that someone — somewhere — will give my son the long awaited miracle he so deserves in his own personal struggle.

Chapter 1

BIRTH AND THE EARLY YEARS

My youngest son was born October 6, 1969, while I was in graduate school, working on a Master's Degree in Guidance and Counseling. I went into labor in the classroom at the university. My husband and a state trooper rushed me to the hospital, and we arrived only minutes before K.P.'s birth.

The next morning, not knowing that he was born with a respiratory infection, I kept asking to see my baby. My husband and the nurse kept telling me he would be brought to me later in the day. Two days later, I discovered that he was born sick and had been transferred to Children's Hospital. I left the hospital after three days, but K.P. stayed for a month, receiving oxygen for twenty-two days.

Going back and forth to the hospital while still assuming my household responsibilities and graduate studies, I soon began to have the post-partum blues. In November, my precious baby came home to meet his two brothers, and my work really started. When he was released from the hospital, we were told he was fine and to treat him like a normal child. However, from the beginning I knew my son, K.P., was different. He cried a lot and never slept at night.

Household responsibilities, my studies, a new baby and lack of rest made me even more depressed. It was very difficult to complete my program, care for a baby and rear two other sons. K.P. was not a planned pregnancy, and I felt pressed to continue my studies since I was on sabbatical from my job as a teacher. I have always been an early morning person, rising around

1

2:00 a.m. to study, complete my assignments and tend to household chores. I would return to bed around 4:30 a.m. and was up again at 6:00 a.m. to feed K.P. and to get his brothers' breakfast ready. I was not letting my children leave home without eating a hot breakfast. My nerves were so bad by the time K.P. was six months old that the doctor prescribed the tranquilizer Valium to relax me. With the grace of God I made it through. K.P. was my bundle of joy, even through these difficult times.

Finally, in May 1970, I graduated. I was very happy about my graduation because this meant more time for K.P. I continued to care for him and returned to work as a guidance counselor in September.

We moved from Washington, D.C. to the suburbs of Rockville, Maryland when K.P. was about eighteen months old. We enrolled him in a regular nursery school program. After two weeks, the director said that something was wrong with him and that he did not fit in with the other children. We were told that he could no longer attend.

Thus began a long series of psychological evaluations at several different medical centers. Test results suggested that K.P. be given time to develop. I was told not to be an overly anxious parent.

When K.P. was two years old, he was referred to the Easter Seal Center for evaluation. These results revealed that he was not developing mentally and that he also had a speech and language problem. At that time the center did not label him as mentally retarded because people were careful not to label children in the seventies. He was accepted at the Easter Seal Center in their pre-school program for speech and language development. After six months or so, we were called in for a conference and told that they no longer could keep K.P. because his behavior was too aggressive and inappropriate (scratching, biting and kicking). We were told that he was acting like an animal. The staff member used no sugar-coated words to describe K.P.'s behavior. Hearing this was very distressing, especially since we had hoped that the Easter Seal Center would be able to provide more answers for K.P.'s problems. I was hurting inside and, of course, I cried.

Chapter 2

SPECIAL SCHOOLS ATTENDED

K.P. was referred to another school for the handicapped. He was then evaluated by the National Children's Center of Washington, D.C. and diagnosed as mentally retarded. He was accepted in the pre-school program, and his tuition was paid by the county government. This was the beginning of my nineteen-year courtship with the Special Education Department of Montgomery County, Maryland. K.P. stayed in school at the National Children's Center until he was eleven. At that time he was doing well and making progress, even though he was not reading and writing.

We decided to have him evaluated by the Kennedy Institute of Washington, D.C., where he was accepted into their program. K.P. stayed at the Kennedy Institute for two years before we were told that he was not making the progress that was expected. They suggested that we consider another placement. We, in turn, went back to the Special Education Department of Montgomery County, where K.P. was given a psychological exam and placed in a county special education school.

He was in that school for one month when I realized that it was not a proper placement for him. K.P. became very aggressive and was going out of control every day (fighting, biting, kicking and running). He did not adjust to the placement at all. I kept telling the principal to refer my son back for an appropriate placement, but for some unknown reason she refused to do so. By then, I was getting calls every day at my job from the assistant principal concerning his behavior. I was asked on several of these calls to pick up K.P. because he had been suspended for his aggressive behavior. Can you imagine suspending a mentally retarded student? On the last suspension, I went to pick up K.P.; I was highly stressed and seeking a solution. I could not convince the principal to refer him back for an appropriate placement. She was certain that eventually he would adjust.

The next morning I wrote a note to the Director of Special Education, gave K.P. his medicine, fixed him a nice bag lunch and took him to the Office of Special Education. And I left him there. This prompted some quick action on the director's behalf. What was she going to do with a mentally disabled young man who was very capable of demolishing her office? I was informed that her coworkers transported K.P. to his school. I had to make a drastic statement, hoping such action would prompt her to see that we needed to have a hearing on his placement.

After more days of battling and protesting with the Special Education Office to re-evaluate K.P.'s placement at the county school, he was sent back to the National Children's Center in a level five or day school placement. The real reason the county tried to keep him in one of their special education schools was to save money. They had to pay the tuition for a private placement. K.P. was happy to return to the National Children's Center. He stayed there until he was twenty-one years old. (After the age of twenty-one, special education was no longer mandated for the handicapped under Public Law 94-142.)

Even this stay was not without a struggle for K.P. and our family. He was doing fine and making some progress. The aggressive behavior began to disappear somewhat. Then it happened! At age fourteen he had a grand mal seizure and had to be placed on an anticonvulsive medication. He was given Dilantin and went out of control, exhibiting explosive behavior every day while on this medication. The doctors changed the medication to Tegretal, and he still had outbursts almost daily. Finally, he was placed on Depakote and began experiencing fewer uncontrolled behavioral incidents.

In addition, we experimented with different psychotropic drugs,[1] such as Haldol and Klonopine. This was to no avail. These medications did not decrease the violent episodes. It has always been my belief that anticonvulsive medications elicited his out of control behavior. K.P.'s system is very sensitive to these medications, even though they controlled his seizures. K.P.'s seizures were all nocturnal, but he still continued to get violent and sometimes had to be restrained. It was very apparent that he could no longer be kept at home. He was accepted in the residential program of his day school placement.

For a while he was doing well. He was now eighteen and had not had a violent outburst in almost two years. The doctor decided to discontinue his anticonvulsive medication to see if he was still epileptic. It was during this time that his father and I decided we should try to maintain K.P. at home. Since he was getting older and stronger, we knew this would probably be our last chance to try to keep him with us. We decided to take him out of the residential program and bring him home. Even though K.P.'s father and I were divorced at that time, we agreed that he should return home to help care for K.P. Both of us were willing to make any sacrifice necessary because we loved him so much.

---

[1] *Psychotropic drugs are drugs that effect the psychic function, behavior or experience.*

Chapter 3

TRYING TO KEEP K.P. AT HOME

Everything went well for about eight months. Then one day the inevitable happened--K.P. had a seizure. He had to be placed on an anticonvulsive medication again and started going out of control at least once a month. It was like a cycle. To track his behavior, we started keeping a daily log. We noticed his demeanor would change in twenty-five to thirty days. This behavior went on for another year. K.P. had to be restrained at times. He began attacking his father and throwing furniture. For some reason, the television was his favorite thing to throw. He would also throw other objects through windows. It seemed that he just had to hear the sound of breaking glass. I knew we had to make a decision about him again. I was also concerned about his father's health. He was restraining and struggling with K.P. who is as strong as three men when he is "out". We knew K.P. could not go back into the residential program at the National Children's Center in Washington, D.C.; however, he was still in the day school program at the Center.

At this point, I didn't know where to turn. K.P. was getting worse and needed help. My family also needed relief from the stress of caregiving. No one would take him (not even for respite) because people were afraid of him. My health was at risk from trying to maintain K.P. I began having heart palpitations due to stress. I had become emotionally, physically and mentally exhausted. If K.P. went out of control when I was alone at home, I would have to call 911. On one 911 call, I told the dispatcher that he was out of control, and I gave them his age and size. They sent a fire truck, police officers and paramedics. My end of the block was literally closed off. As a result, everyone in the neighborhood knew K.P. was out of control.

I remember so vividly the afternoon he "went off". When I picked up K.P. from school that day, I knew he was disturbed, but I was trying to make it home with him. He began pushing the buttons in the car, moving his seat back and forth and jamming his knees into the dashboard. He was screaming and exhibiting self-injurious behavior all the way home--ten miles. I felt I was losing it, even though I was talking to him while driving, telling him "You are going to be all right." When we arrived home, all hell broke loose. K.P.'s screaming and yelling escalated. He began beating his fists on the walls. Luckily his oldest brother, Jim, was home at the time, and I called to him to come upstairs. K.P. had gone into the kitchen, thrown the television on top of the stove, knocked over the table and was throwing chairs around. Jim restrained him, and we called an ambulance to take him to the hospital.

We had to make a decision as to what to do with K.P. In the past we always brought him home from the emergency room after he had been given a mild sedative. This time Jim and I knew that we could not bring K.P. home. He desperately needed help. What do we do now?

The hospital sent a social worker and a nurse in to talk with us. They tried to get K.P. scheduled for an evaluation at another hospital; unfortunately, the hospital did not have a room available. Other facilities were contacted, but there was no place to send him. My son and I asked the social worker what would happen if we left K.P. in the emergency room. He explained that the Department of Social Services would be called in, and I would lose the rights I had as K.P.'s parent. This act would be considered abandonment. I asked, "Would he get the help that is needed?" He stated that Social Services would be notified, and they would have to find a place for him. After an hour of thinking about our options, my oldest son said to me, "Mom, you really don't have a choice. He needs help." We decided to leave K.P. strapped down in the emergency room.

Chapter 4

THE ABANDONMENT

I ABANDONED MY SON! Even though he was nineteen, leaving him was the hardest decision of my life. I couldn't sleep that night. The pain was unbearable knowing that K.P. was strapped down and lying on his back in the emergency room for almost twenty-four hours. What else could I do? I felt helpless, but knew that this would get him the help he so desperately needed. I called the nurses every hour to check on him. The social worker from the Department of Social Services called me the next morning, asking for K.P.'s records. She wanted to know more about him. Jim took a copy of all the records (medical reports, psychologicals and school records) to the hospital for the social worker. Around 6:00 p.m. that evening, she called again, asking if a family member could come and stay with K.P. for the night because they wanted to unstrap him. His brother went to stay with him. Before he left the next morning, they had to strap K.P. down again, even though he was calm. The hospital did not have the personnel to watch him around the clock.

That morning, the Department of Social Services was going before the judge to have K.P. committed to the Great Oaks Center for the mentally disabled in Silver Spring, Maryland.

From this legal action, K.P. was placed in Great Oaks where he could receive the help he needed. At the time we made the decision to abandon K.P., I didn't know that the abandonment would short circuit the five-year waiting list that his name was on for alternative living.

K.P. immediately became eligible for many services. The judge later appointed me his legal guardian, after reports were made on what a good parent I was to K.P. Two days after the planned abandonment, I saw K.P. at Great Oaks. He did not see me, however. I was there to meet with the staff and provide them with more information on K.P. He was walking across the campus with three other clients and a counselor. After seeing him that time, I did not see him face to face for a month. I was advised to give him time to adjust to Great Oaks. I knew if I went to visit him he would throw a tantrum and say "I want to go home, Mama." His oldest brother, Jim, visited him weekly. We knew he wouldn't get upset with him. Jim kept me informed on how K.P. was adjusting. While living at Great Oaks, he was transported to his day school placement at the National Children's Center in Washington, D.C. I would visit his school weekly on my lunch hour to observe him through a one-way mirror. Each time was painful, knowing I could not speak to him. However, I was elated to see that he was being cared for properly. Finally, when he saw me at Great Oaks after four weeks, his eyes were as large as fifty-cent pieces because he knew he was going home with Mama for his first weekend visit.

Great Oaks was a different kind of environment for K.P., but he adjusted. I really liked Great Oaks as a home for him. There were so many activities going on--dances, hayrides, cookouts--but the goal of Great Oaks was to prepare clients for alternative living.

One day the call came that they had a group home placement for K.P. I didn't want him to live in the group home, but after much thought I decided that he should be given a chance to live in a community again. I was afraid that he would be difficult to manage in a home when he became violent and eventually would have to return to Great Oaks. I did not want him to go through another change, but he moved into the group home after all. Everything went well for a while. Then came a change of employees. It seems as though it is difficult to keep good, stable employees in residential programs. I felt that the agency was not monitoring the employees as closely as they should. His program called for weekly exercise, but K.P. wasn't getting it. As a result, his weight went from 194 pounds to 201 pounds in only four weeks due to improper diet and lack of exercise.

When K.P. came home on the weekends, he was kept on a regular exercise program. We would take him swimming, biking and walking. He played kickball. Unfortunately, I had to stop bringing him home because he began having outbursts at home on the weekends. During the last weekend visit in September 1991, K.P.'s counselor came home with him in the event that he had to be restrained. At a nearby playground he got away from the counselor and threw a brick through a neighbor's window. Fortunately, no one was hurt. In our attempt to take him back to the group home, he hit me on my head with his fists several times while I was driving. I saw stars and almost passed out, but did manage to stop the car after he pushed the gear in reverse. K.P. knew directions, and he wanted me to turn the car around and head home. He kept saying "Go that way." We were lucky that there were no cars behind us. The counselor was in the car, and after some talking to K.P., we were able to get him back to the group home.

After this incident, the weekend trips were discontinued for six months. Even though I visited K.P. every Thursday, it was very painful for both of us that he was no longer coming home. I continued to wash and iron his clothes and take goodies to him. I was in therapy for six weeks to deal with the pain of separation since I couldn't bring him home.

During this period, I was also house hunting in Petersburg, Virginia, trying hard to find a house with a large backyard for K.P. After the brick throwing incident, it was my intention not to bring him back to the neighborhood where he had lived for 20 years.

Sometimes K.P. would protest his not being able to come home by throwing tantrums when I visited him. This was very upsetting to me. I was told he had crying spells at his job site. I knew K.P. was depressed because he was not coming home to enjoy his weekend visits.

After six months, I decided to start bringing him home again. I had found a new home in Virginia for the family. K.P. was so very happy to be coming to his new home, although he would still ask about the house in Maryland. We resumed our activities together: swimming, biking, kickball and eating out. K.P. was very happy and so was I. He said to me "I am happy to be home, sleeping in my bed. I love you, Mama."

Chapter 5

DIAGNOSIS AND DOCUMENTED BEHAVIORAL PATTERNS

K.P.'s psychologicals revealed that his major handicapping condition appears to be severe to profound mental retardation, complicated by a severe language disorder and aggressive behavior. His episodes of maladaptive behavior include aggression, self injury and property destruction. K.P.'s adaptive behaviors include self-care tasks, oral hygiene, domestic skills, communication skills and sports activities. He is learning proper expression of anger and frustration and functions on a four-to-five-year-old level.

It was helpful to keep a log of K.P.'s actions. This way we could determine if there was a consistent pattern of behavior. At one time his out-of-control behavior was happening every thirty days or so. The following behavior pattern was recorded in 1987, when K.P. was eighteen and living at home:

01/07	Seizure
03/01	Screaming; very noncompliant
03/04	Noncompliant
03/07	Very little screaming
03/10	Aggressive behavior; hitting student at school
03/21	Screaming
03/24	Destruction of property at school
05/08	Had to be restrained
05/09	Yelling at school; desk banging

05/10	Time out room
05/16	Threw student walker
05/17	Aggressive; safety coat and time out room
05/18	Very "off" last night; slept very little
06/29	Aggressive behavior; had to be restrained
07/21	Aggressive behavior; had to be restrained
08/18	Aggressive
11/10	Seizure
11/16	Aggressive behavior
12/12	Non-compliant at home and school

On the days where you see no entry of behavior, he was usually very good.

Chapter 6

THE EFFECTS OF PSYCHOTROPIC DRUGS

In our struggle to help K.P. and keep him home, we tried many different drugs to prevent him from going out of control. Unfortunately, K.P. would always be in that percentage of those who would suffer side effects from prescribed drugs. The following is a list of psychotropic drugs used, along with the side effects they had on K.P.:

Haldol	Swelling of chest (gynecomastia)
Halcain	Stupor, spaced out
Klonopine	Increased explosive behavior
Thorazine	Drowsy, nervous
Serentil	Increased explosive behavior
Zoloft	Increased explosive behavior
Mellaril	Self-injurious behavior (bending fingers back, pushing in eyes)

We continued to experiment with other psychotropic drugs in an attempt to lessen K.P.'s violent outbursts. We had hoped that maybe one day we would find a drug that would assist him in his struggle. (He feels so badly after an episode; he believes that you are upset with him for having one. I always assure him: "It's O.K., K.P., it's O.K. Let it out of your system. I love you." He responds, simply, "It's O.K.")

These violent outbursts often come without any indication. Sometimes you can tell by looking at his eyes. They may get a little red. Usually, he starts with self-injurious behavior; some intervention must be taken immediately. K.P. is often restrained at this point. He is currently being trained to wrap himself in a blanket at the onset of these episodes. Afterwards, you must watch him closely because he will stick objects, like a pencil or toothbrush, down his throat to make himself vomit. He was restricted from wearing a belt for this reason. K.P. recognizes when he is about to have an episode. He tries so hard to suppress it and starts talking to himself: "K.P. must stay in control. You don't bite. You don't scratch. You don't scream. You don't hit. You must be a fine young man." He has learned to use expressive therapy to help control his violent outbursts.

Recently, when it appeared he was about to have an episode, he went out onto the patio and began to jump up and down. The jumping continued for a few minutes. Then the counselor joined in and transformed the jumping into an exercise routine. This seemed to calm K.P. His energy was redirected to prevent an emotional outburst.

In October 1995, K.P. was admitted to the Epilepsy Center at the University of Maryland Hospital in Baltimore. He was in the monitoring unit for one week. It was determined that his outbursts were more behavior-related than seizure-related. When he was discharged, Zoloft was prescribed for him. This drug did not help K.P. at all. As a matter of fact, three weeks later, he was admitted to another hospital for five days after having more outbursts of behavioral episodes. He was then taken off Zoloft and put on Mellaril. This drug did not help either. He was then taken off Mellaril and Risperdal was prescribed. Currently, he is still on Risperdal, although this medication is not working. The duration and frequency of his outbursts gets worse as K.P. gets older. I'm afraid for him, afraid that his heart will not continue to take the stress of these episodes.

Before K.P. was accepted in the National Children Center's residential program, he was sent to Springfield Mental Health Adolescent Center for a ten-day observation. He was then sent to a behavioral management program at the Walter P. Carter Center in Baltimore for thirty days, after which he was accepted in the residential program of his day school placement. K.P. was still taking an anticonvulsive medication. One day we went to visit K.P., and we noticed some bedroom furniture totally smashed to pieces. I remarked to K.P.'s brother, "Look at that! K.P. did that." We asked the staff what had happened to the furniture, and they said "The new patient, K.P., smashed it. He is very strong!" "Oh, yes, that's my son," I responded.

Chapter 7

RELATIONSHIP WITH FAMILY MEMBERS

K.P.'s brothers were very supportive of him, particularly my middle son, Jerry. Jerry was still living at home when K.P. was there. He was always there to help out in any way he could, even with all of his responsibilities in school. Jerry became my source of emotional strength and support. To this day, I have never heard him complain in any way about K.P., although I can imagine what it was like for him. We have all accepted K.P. as he is and love him. Maybe one day Jerry will share his thoughts in a book, too.

K.P.'s relationship with each of his brothers was very different. He would physically attack his Dad or Jerry at any time. I never recall Jerry striking him back. Jerry and K.P. played together. They always shared their birthday parties, since K.P.'s birthday is October 6th and Jerry's is October 9th. Jerry is five years older than his brother. As K.P. got older, he became jealous of Jerry. He did not want me to talk to his brother, wanting all of my attention for himself.

K.P. was very different with his oldest brother, Jim, and me. I think, perhaps, we were his strongest disciplinarians, and he knew his limits with both of us. His father's inability to control K.P.'s behavior put an excessive amount of stress on me. It became apparent that our faltering, abusive marriage could not survive, so we decided to separate when K.P. was ten years old.

There has always been a special bond between K.P. and me. We are very sensitive to each other's emotional state. I can always feel when he is in pain or when he is not sleeping. I can feel and sense his problems. K.P. can also sense my presence. If I leave home when he is in his room sleeping, he wakes up and comes downstairs.

One way K.P. and I would bond was by dressing alike. For instance, if we went shopping and I bought a sweat suit for him, I would buy one for myself in the same color. K.P.'s favorite color is navy blue. We have vests and tennis shoes alike, and he really loves this idea. His brothers always buy two pieces of the same clothing, one for K.P. and one for me. K.P. is not very verbal, but he would say "K.P. and Mom, the same color," and point to his sweat suit and then to mine.

K.P. is like any other human being in terms of feelings. In our family, we are very affectionate. K.P. often comes to me and hugs me or other family members. I shudder to think how K.P. would have been if he did not know how much we love him. He knows that he is loved. Most family decisions revolve around K.P. This is my way of holding the family together and keeping everyone in touch with him.

To try to reassure K.P. of my love for him, I would place my hand over my heart and say, "You are very close to my heart, I love you." My son is echolalic, which means that he repeats words that are spoken to him. He would echo back to me, "You are very close to my heart, I love you."

There are so many happy moments with K.P. He has a good demeanor when he is not out of control. He loves being funny. After my divorce, I focused most of my attention on K.P. Everything I did was for him. The other children had grown up and were leaving for college. They no longer needed or wanted pampering from me. Due to K.P.'s condition, I could continue to pamper him. His brother, Jerry, called him Prince, because he said I treated him like a prince. I became K.P.'s advocate, fighting for proper placement and hiring a lawyer to help get the funding needed for his schooling, which he was entitled to under Public Law 94-142 for the handicapped.

Chapter 8

LIFE WITH K.P.

There are so many more experiences that I could include in this book. It seems as though I've only touched the tip of an iceberg. There were many times that it seemed just impossible to maintain K.P. at home; I was raising two other children at the same time. K.P. was extremely hyperactive and his doctor suggested trying phenobarbital. This was a terrible experience for K.P. He was up all night roaming the house. The medication made him even more hyperactive; in turn, he was taken off phenobarbital.

Because of his hyperactivity, we considered putting him in a residential school in Pennsylvania. (He was then seven or eight years old.) We went to visit the school which was a residential program for hyperactive children. K.P.'s application and records were sent as requested. While we were being interviewed, K.P. dashed out of the building like a bolt of lightning. We all searched for over an hour and could not find him. Eventually, he was found sitting inside a large drain pipe. Of course, you can guess the outcome. K.P. was not accepted at the school. We were told that the school did not have the personnel to provide K.P. with the kind of individual assistance he needed.

There were also interviews at other schools, but to no avail. They all said they could not accept K.P. because he required a lot of one-on-one attention, and the schools were not staffed to provide that type of service. The schools were also concerned about K.P.'s safety. We got the impression that since K.P. did not respond to medication for hyperactivity in a positive way, they could not accept him. In many cases, these kids who are on medication have positive results, while K.P. has never responded well to certain drugs.

When K.P. was younger (five to ten years of age), he was a runner. He would just take off and run. This could happen at home, at school or just about anywhere. Often he would run to his bedroom, slam the door and trash his room. There were times he would be lost for an hour or more. He was so quick and fast it was difficult to catch up with him, or to see in which direction he had run. I will never forget the day he dashed out of the front door, ran into a neighbor's house, and took a seat at their dining room table. The neighbors knew K.P., so they gave him some cookies and came outside to tell me he was in their house.

By the time K.P. was eleven or twelve, he had grown out of his hyperactive behavior. I started taking him with me to the eight o'clock Sunday morning church service because it was short. We would visit friends and even go to small parties. He was well behaved and handsome in his dress clothes. We always bought very nice clothes for him and kept him well groomed. We knew by keeping his appearance clean, he would be accepted more easily by others. He independently brushes his teeth, washes and dries his hands, and with some prompting, he can brush his hair. He is very neat, independently performing all toileting, dressing and eating skills. K.P. maintains a neat and tidy room; he likes to keep his things in place.

I remember when K.P. was in a placement that wasn't appropriate for him. We had been to several hearings, trying to speed up the process to secure private school funding. People were dragging their feet, and I couldn't go to work for days because I had to take care of K.P. at home. Some days I had someone wait in the car with him while I worked for an hour. While we were waiting for a decision to be made on the funding, I took K.P. to the Maryland State Department of Education office, Division of Special Education in Baltimore and took a seat. I refused to move and demanded that I see the director. At that time, many people came out to talk with me, saying that they were doing the best they could on K.P.'s case. I kept my posture and still demanded to see the director. Finally, an hour later, he came to talk with me. He assured me that they would speed up the decision on K.P.'s case. Satisfied with our meeting, we left his office and headed back to Rockville, Maryland, which is about a half-hour drive from Baltimore.

By the time we got home, my telephone was ringing as I walked through the door. It was the Special Education Department in Rockville, telling me K.P.'s funding had been approved and that we should report to their office the next morning. They stated they had heard that K.P. and I had visited the main office. They wanted to know what had happened in Baltimore, and what I had said to get the funding approved so quickly.

From this experience I found out that I had to fight to get proper funding and appropriate placement for my child. As I stated previously, I have been and continue to be his advocate, being very vocal on his behalf. Being vocal has not made me a popular person with some agencies, but I don't apologize for being a concerned parent.

While K.P. was in Great Oaks, he went to his day school placement, the National Children's Center, by van. He enjoyed going to school because there were so many interesting activities going on, including being taught such basic personal information as writing his name, age, where he lived and his parents' names. In prevocational training, he learned to do many tasks: preparing pizza boxes, stuffing envelopes and preparing cups with health aids for health care centers. He was also taught survival skills. However, it is very difficult for him to stay on task because of his Attention Deficit Disorder (ADD). The one thing he likes to do best is to put clothes in the washing machine and dryer. He can fold the clothes and put them where they belong. He can also identify each piece of clothing and to whom it belongs. He like to wash clothes with Woolite because it is liquid. He always checks to see if I have some. When we go to the supermarket, he finds a bottle and puts it in the shopping cart, saying "Woolite, Mama, Woolite." I think K.P. likes to be in the laundry room because he has a fascination with water. He loves to play in water and will pour out anything liquid. Whenever he comes home, I hide all liquids like dish detergents and leave a small amount of Woolite in the container.

When K.P. graduated from the National Children's Center, he was accepted in a vocational program, also located in Maryland. He has been in the program for five years now and loves it. Some of his vocational training has been stuffing envelopes, packaging toothpaste, toothbrushes, combs, etc. for health care centers and removing the casings around cassette tapes. He is paid for performing these tasks. Even though he cannot count money, K.P. is aware that money is needed to buy things. When he goes to the barber shop, we always give him money to pay for his haircut. He knows how to tip the barber, too. Then he gives me the thumbs-up sign to indicate that everything is fine.

My life changed over the years to adapt to K.P.'s condition. I did not want to risk his going out of control with guests in the house, so I celebrated all holidays as "pre-holidays": a pre-Thanksgiving dinner, a pre-Christmas party. All of my social activities and entertaining were done before bringing K.P. home for the holidays or weekends. It was always important to have him home on the holidays, not only for his benefit, but to give the counselors at the group home an opportunity to be with their loved ones, too. I soon learned to coordinate and work as a team with the counselors. It was always to K.P.'s advantage and mine to develop and maintain a good relationship with the staff.

When my son was younger, we used to go to the amusement park every weekend during the summer. He enjoyed the rides, especially the water rides. We spent most Sundays having fun. His father and brother would go with us occasionally. As K.P. got older, he didn't like the rides anymore. He refused to go on them. It seemed that his fear of the rides had gotten to him. However, he would ride the merry-go-round with me. K.P. enjoyed the pizza and ice cream at the amusement park. He loved to eat there and always looked forward to feasting whenever we went to the park.

In later years, I have noticed that K.P. has become uncomfortable in crowds. He will cling to my arm, not letting go and not wanting to stay. This uncomfortable behavior is also shown when we go to crowded malls. He seems to function best in a one-on-one situation. He does enjoy going places, however. If I attempt to leave or just talk about going somewhere, he says, "I'm going with Mama." He will not stay with anyone else when I am present.

On the weekends when K.P. comes home, he always says, "I stay home, no more group home. Just me and you, Mama." For many months this was the way it was, just K.P. and I. He did so much to help me maintain my balance. I would lose myself in caring for him and all of my other problems were temporarily blanked out.

I did not think of myself or other concerns. I stayed focused on caring for my son.

In some ways this caregiving was and is an emotional outlet for me. There were times I hated to see him return to the group home because I had to return to reality and face any problems that I might have. I became his favorite playmate because we were always alone. Many times I felt I was reliving my childhood. It was like being a kid again. I, too, always looked forward to our bike riding, swimming, kickball and other activities we so much enjoyed. My commitment to K.P. was and is like a marriage. I am committed to him "for better or worse, for richer or poorer, in sickness and in health, 'til death do us part."

Tending to K.P. did not interfere with completing my graduate studies. I continued to go to school. His two brothers and Dad helped to take care of him. I had my career as a guidance counselor and worked a part-time evening job as a counselor for twelve years. I never could accumulate leave time on the job, since I would use most of it for K.P.'s medical appointments, or for attending conferences. They were all scheduled during the day. There were times I had to take off from work simply for rest and relaxation before picking up K.P. from school. Even though I did not have other family members, I knew with proper planning my other sons and K.P.'s dad would take care of him. My middle son, Jerry, eventually became my support system. He attended hearings and conferences and took a primary interest in K.P. At one time, it was just the three of us at home, and we were there to help each other. Jerry could feel and see my struggle. I had no one to turn to but him and my outside support group. When he was home, K.P.'s brother and I talked a lot. In light of K.P.'s jealousy, Jerry and I did not talk as much in front of him. When Jerry left for college, so did my family support system. He was all I had. I felt so help-less, thinking to myself, "What am I going to do now with no family at all to depend upon?" Jerry did not realize how dependent I was upon him. Being in this position strengthened my faith in God's helping hand.

It has been very difficult for me, but I had the faith and courage to keep going. K.P.'s dad was not part of his life for three years. Even though his father could not manage him that well, he was good with the custodial care. When he did return after three years to see K.P., we had a lot of anxiety as to how K.P. would react towards him. I'll never forget the look on his face when his dad and I went to pick him up for a weekend visit. His expression seemed to say, "Where did he come from, Mom?" He accepted his father just like he had always been there. His dad asked, "Who am I, K.P.?" "Daddy," he replied. His response made his father very happy.

To keep informed about my son's problem, I took classes in special education, read books relating to his condition and surrounded myself with people knowledgeable about mental disabilities. I always asked a lot of questions, trying to keep informed on the latest, most progressive techniques and current programs that could benefit K.P. and his condition. I was very involved in all of K.P.'s programs. I made regular weekly visits to his school to check on his progress. I always took K.P. to his annual school dance. Handsomely dressed, he enjoyed the music and dancing. He had so much fun dancing with and talking to the staff and his classmates.

Several times a week when K.P. was in the residential program at school and in the group home, I drove there to tidy up his room before going to work. In order not to upset him, I was careful to make certain he had gone to school or to his vocational training. This gave me the motherly feeling of still caring for him. While I was there, I also checked his clothes and closet, straightened out drawers and made certain socks and underclothes were where they belonged. I always left some goodies like a piece of fruit or candy on the pillow for him.

As a guidance counselor, I began to realize that I had much to share with other parents, particularly parents who cannot accept the fact that their child has a problem. I am sharing my experience with them in hope that it serves as a wake-up call for them, helping them to realize how fortunate they are if they can recognize the positive aspects of such a parental experience. Having a child like K.P. has helped to make me a better person. I am more compassionate, sympathetic and caring of other people and their problems.

There were times when I acted like a comedian, laughing and telling jokes to others. I developed a sense of humor and learned to laugh at most anything. This was my way of coping and releasing stress. Whenever my other two sons and I were together, there was much laughter. They, too, have developed a sense of humor. Laughter and humor are very therapeutic.

No story is complete without some humor. One day K.P.'s oldest brother took him to a department store. After being in the store a few minutes, the sales clerk came over to his brother and said, "Hey, you know the guy who came in the store with you? He's over there standing on his head." His brother responded, "Don't worry about it, he does it all the time."

Chapter 9

K.P. TODAY

Presently, K.P. is twenty-six years old and resides in an alternative-living home in Maryland with two other clients. These guys have been together for six years and are very much a family. There are counselors on duty twenty-four hours a day. This is the second group home K.P. has lived in. After living at the first group home for about two years, K.P. had an episode one morning while eating breakfast. He suddenly dashed out the side door, ran into a neighbor's yard, and threw a pot through the neighbor's front glass door before a counselor could intervene. An elderly couple living in that house was horrified. This incident caused quite a stir in the community. The couple's children were very upset and complained to the agency and other county officials. After this episode, someone stated that K.P. could get hurt because he does not look like he is disabled, and as a result, he could be held accountable for his actions. This incident got the group evicted from that particular house, and they moved to their present living site.

K.P. is in a day vocational training program, and a van picks him up daily, taking him to the training site. He enjoys the van ride very much, and it helps to make his day. A behavioral specialist is working with him on a weekly basis at the vocational training center.

K.P. continues to visit his family every other weekend in Virginia. He tolerates the two-and-a-half hour ride very well. We plan many activities, and he has so much fun; he usually sleeps all the way back to Maryland.

In researching the services for the handicapped in my area of Virginia, there were none comparable to the services he was receiving in Maryland. Even if there was a comparable program in Virginia, it would not be in K.P.'s best interest to relocate him. He is well adjusted to his present arrangement and friends. A change could have a devastating effect on him. Change is very difficult, especially for people like K.P. By providing proper training and keeping him in the community, my primary goal for him is to be as independent as possible. Isn't that what all parents want for their children?

K.P. is also very athletic and strong. He has broad shoulders and is well built. Sports are his major interest, and I know he would have been a good football player. When he was in school, he participated in the Special Olympics events of swimming, running track, and shooting basketball. He is an excellent swimmer and has won many gold medals. He owes his good swimming skills to his father. By the time K.P. was two, we realized he was not afraid of water and that it was very therapeutic for him. We, in turn, had a pool installed at our Maryland home. His father would put him in the pool with a life jacket on. As a result, K.P. learned to swim at an early age. He also likes listening to music, dancing and riding his bike. In later years, he developed an interest in drawing and in building with Lego blocks. K.P. has a mechanical mind. He can operate every appliance in the home, including the microwave.

Chapter 10

SOCIETY'S ATTITUDE TOWARD THE MENTALLY DISABLED

Many people, including my own father, thought having a child like K.P. was God's way of punishing you for the wrong you had done to someone else. Before he died, my Dad asked me, "Baby, have you ever mistreated anyone? Have you ever done anything bad to anyone?" It is amazing what some people think about the mentally disabled and how uninformed they are about them. Society is to blame for this lack of knowledge. For many years, society did not accept the mentally retarded. They were hidden, maltreated, and even locked away.

Society still does not give justice to the disabled. There has been a change in attitude, and some progress has been made in recent years. There is still this "what a shame" attitude, however. Those are the worst words anyone could say to me about my son. "What a shame" does not describe K.P. and others like him at all. There is no time to think "what a shame"; rather, one must seek available resources. There is also a need for more research and in-depth study. Of course, there are programs and schools, and much has been accomplished under previous legislation (Public Law 94-142) and the present Individuals with Disabilities Education Act.

When I was a child, my grandparents would take me to visit some friends who had reared a mentally retarded child with their children. I vividly remember that this young lady was not allowed to come into the house while company was there. She was made to stay outside, down by the edge of the woods. During that time, people kept their mentally retarded children a secret hidden "in the closet". Today's society has changed somewhat. More often than in the past, the mentally disabled are made to feel loved by their families and accepted as part of society. There are special education programs for them and activities such as the Special Olympics. K.P. was very fortunate to live in a county where funding was available. He has always been in the best programs. This is due, in part, to my being his advocate and fighting so hard for him.

However, there is still so much that needs to be explored to help relieve the agony suffered by individuals like K.P. I appeal to those in the medical field to find a "miracle".

Chapter 11

MY FAITH IN GOD

There are times when I wonder, "Why me Lord? Why me?" However, I know God only gives you what you can bear. Sometimes the cross gets very heavy, but you must continue the journey. There are periods of time when I must pray more for K.P., so I burn a candle every night for thirty days and pray during the middle of the night for him. It seems as though my prayers are better heard in the stillness of the night. My experience with K.P. has been a test of faith.

One night, I received a call from the nurse at the agency for the group home. K.P. had been taken to the hospital for pushing his hand through the window pane in his bedroom. I was hysterical. I did not know what to do. I threatened to sue the agency for letting this happen. Not being able to visit K.P. made things worse. He was not receptive to visits from family unless we were taking him home. Our presence would make it worse for the staff to handle him. (He always wants to come home, and whenever he sees me, he thinks he is going home.) I prayed to God he would not have a serious injury. I couldn't sleep until I heard from the hospital. Finally, I was told that he received ten stitches and had been seen by a psychiatrist. He was released back to the group home. How frightening this must have been for him. I was happy that the injury wasn't any worse. Where does one get the resiliency to keep going? From Almighty God, who continues to give me strength.

Often I felt as if I couldn't go on. Where could I turn? The only emotional support I had came from my middle son, my support group and some friends who were very close to me. My husband, at that time, was not supportive, psychologically or emotionally. He could never say anything comforting and was physically and verbally abusive. I thought, dear Lord, just put someone in my life who understands what I am going through.

Although God grants us the opportunity to parent and rear children to the age of reason, there are some He leaves with us for a lifetime, perpetual children to love and comfort perhaps for reasons only He knows. So we give them our love, and most often, the love they give us back is pure and childlike, even after they are "adults". When K.P. is at his best, he gives pure love... and it is truly cherished.

Chapter 12

SOME SUGGESTIONS FOR ACCEPTING AND CARING FOR A LOVED ONE WITH A DISABILITY

1. Recognize and accept that there is a problem with your loved one.
2. Seek professional help. See a specialist in the appropriate field of medicine.
3. Get a second opinion.
4. Begin having the problem treated.
5. Research the problem and become very knowledgeable about the disability.
6. Continue to show the disabled how much you love them.
7. Become an advocate for your loved one; fight for the best of care and do whatever it takes.
8. Investigate other custodial care facilities for respite and find out what home services are available. You will need a break.
9. Maintain a good relationship with your higher power.
10. Exercise often to help relieve stress and tension.
11. Add humor to your life. Laughter and humor are good stress reducers.
12. Join a support group.

Chapter 13

ENTRIES FROM K.P.'S BABY BOOK

K.P.'s Birth Announcement
Date of Birth: October 6, 1969
Place of Birth: Washington Hospital Center
Washington, D.C.
Color of Hair: Black
Color of Eyes: Brown
Complexion: Medium Brown
Weight: 7 and ¾ pounds

When K.P. First...
Smiled: March 1970
Showed a tooth: March 1970 (two teeth)
Said a word: November 1971 "Mom"

K.P.'s First Birthday and Other Events

October 6, 1970	Put both hands in his birthday cake.
October 7, 1971	Urinated in the toilet for the first time.
May 2, 1972	Won't take his bottle any more.

K.P.'s First and Other Christmases

December 1969	K.P. loved the lights on the tree. He would not play with his stuffed animals at first.

December 1970	Still likes the lights on the tree, but would not get on his rocking horse.
December 1971	Really enjoyed Christmas this year. He played with his brother's toys.
December 1974	K.P. is getting along fine. He is repeating what you say to him. He is aware of Santa, but still not very alert.

Early Trips

| June 1972 | Virginia Beach and Ocean City, Maryland. We went by car. K.P. enjoyed the ride. |
| July 1973 | Disney World, Orlando, Florida. Liked the Disney characters. Tried to touch Mickey Mouse. |

Two Years Old

| October 1971 | K.P. and Jerry had their birthday party together. K.P. slept through the party. |

Three Years Old

| November 1972 | Still cannot say very many words. He can say Mama, Daddy, and his brothers' names. |

Four Years Old

July 23, 1974   In a special school. He still does not talk in sentences, but repeats everything you say to him.

Five Years Old

October 14, 1974   K.P. is a big boy. He can do flips, but still cannot talk in sentences.

December 1974   Attending a special school. His language has improved slightly. He understands certain commands. His behavior is improving slowly.

Six Years Old

December 15, 1975   Still in a special school. He is saying more words. It is very obvious now that he is a special child with a language problem.

Seven Years old

June 25, 1977   Attending the National Children's Center. We are proud of his progress.

Eleven Years Old

January 1980

Now at the Kennedy Institute. He is not as hyperactive as he was. He is learning to be independent. He is counting. I love him dearly and he is making a lot of progress.

Seventeen Years Old

November 1986

K.P. is a big guy now. He is in the residential program at the National Children's Center. His behavior is up and down. Right now "his thing" is screaming in school. He is still the joy of my life. It is so rewarding to be with him on the weekends. He loves coming home. We do a lot of bike riding together. He loves the movies. I think he likes to go to the movies just to eat popcorn.

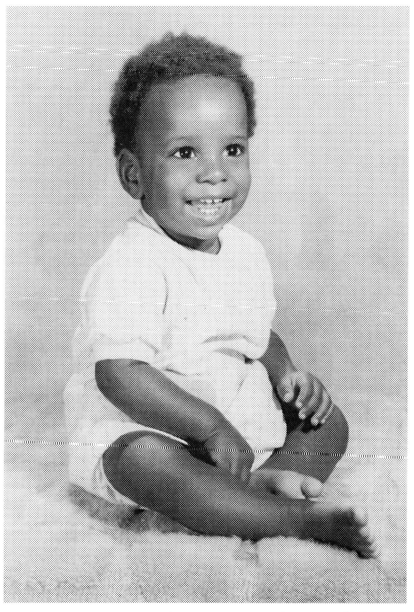

K.P. at six months old

Chapter 14

ANECDOTAL NOTES TAKEN FROM K.P.'S COMMUNICATION BOOK

02/22/88   K.P. did well today, especially considering the sty in his eye. He was irritable, but still did his work at school.

02/23/88   Very slow last evening. He had a seizure at 2:00 a.m.

08/05/88   Went to the public swimming pool today and did great.

08/30/88   Did not sleep last night. The doctor prescribed Mellaril for him. He is showing signs of nervousness; bending his fingers back, confused and agitated.

02/03/89   K.P. was absolutely wonderful in school today! He was in such a good mood and so happy.

02/05/89   Kind of sick this weekend with a cold. He got plenty of rest, chicken soup, and cough syrup. He did get to go out late Sunday for kickball.

06/30/90 — To VSI and TREXLER. K.P. had a good weekend until Sunday at 2:00 p.m., when a fight at the pool excited him. He went out of control and was taken to D.C. General Hospital.

07/07/90 — Home from Wednesday to Friday. His toes are getting better. He is in a good mood today. Had a good week.

07/27/91 — To VSI and TREXLER. Had a good weekend. He was in a very good mood. Glad to know things are going well at VSI.

07/27/91 — Had a good day. I wrote too soon. He had a small incident around noon.

08/13/91 — Came back from the hospital yesterday. O.K. after the incident at VSI. At about 6:00 p.m., he flooded the bathroom at the group home and water dripped down to the basement.

08/24/91 — To VSI. Visited K.P. this afternoon. He appeared sleepy and tired. It was a good visit.

08/21/91 — Had another wonderful day at the workshop. He is going to the Token Store tomorrow.

08/30/91 — Very good day at the workshop and on the van.

09/01/91   To VSI and TREXLER. Very good weekend. He was so good. Had a good week.

09/04/91   Worked all morning but had a slight confrontation with another client at the end of the day.

09/12-16/91   This week started very normal for K.P. There was some aggressive behavior on Tuesday, but he was able to turn things around and the rest of the day went well. On Wednesday morning there was a behavioral incident after he got off the van.

06/15-19/92   What a great week! He was so happy and full of fun. He was able to stay on task at work. On Friday he tried to run out of the front door at the group home.

08/27-31/92   No problems this week. He went to sleep at work after lunch. He must have been tired from his weekend of fun in Petersburg, VA.

09/21-26/92   There was an incident on the van Tuesday morning. He did manage to pull it together and work even though he was still somewhat agitated.

12/21-29/92   K.P. is talking about going home for Christmas. He has a dental appointment on Tuesday at 8:30 a.m. He is doing quite well this week.

01/25-29/93   In a good cycle. Having a great week and staying on task!

04/26-29/93   Excellent week at the group home and worksite. It has been a very productive week for him. He is in an excellent mood.

05/01-02/93   This morning (Saturday) went well for K.P. He went to the zoo with other clients. He saw someone he knew from his former school. He enjoyed looking at the animals.

08/02-06/93   Had a good week until Friday. He trashed his room this evening. Was feeling better by morning.

11/25-28/93   Had a super Thanksgiving at home with his family. He was great! He enjoyed being home and ate and ate and ate.

01/10-14/94   K.P. is having a great week. He is staying on task and working most of the day. He is being compliant and working very hard.

02/01-28/94   February was a good month for K.P. There were no incidents. He was very cooperative and completed most of his work.

03/25/94   K.P. was just a bit upset today, but he calmed down on his own. Very good use of self control.

07/11-15/94	Very good week for K.P. He stayed on task and was compliant. He did a lot of work today.
09/06-09/94	The week started great after the holiday. On Thursday, K.P. was edgy during the morning hours. He did some deep-breathing techniques and calmed himself down. The rest of the week was uneventful.
10/17-21/94	A good week for K.P.; no tantrums, good social interaction. He was very productive this week.
11/28-12/04/94	K.P. had an incident that started to escalate, but he did some deep breathing techniques and did not have to be restrained. The rest of the week was fine.
12/19-23/94	What a great week. K.P. practiced stop breathing techniques and worked on stencils.
1995	*(A noted increase of behavioral outbursts.)*
01/09-13/95	Monday started off great. He did brain talk[1] and followed directions. There was an incident on Tuesday in which he had to be restrained.

[1] *Brain talk is a technique used to associate the left side of the brain with the right side of the brain. An example would be crossing the right arm over the left.*

01/19/95	Incident in the afternoon. Property destruction. Some self-injurious behavior (biting hand and slapping face). Had to be restrained.
01/31/95	K.P. did stencils and brain talk this morning. He had an incident in the afternoon that required some intervention.
02/07/95	Incident today of self injury (scratched his face). He responded to verbal commands.
02/08/95	Self injury and property destruction. Had to be restrained.
2/11-12/95	K.P. had an incident on Saturday; violent outburst. Had to be restrained.
03/15/95	Two incidents today without warning; property destruction. Verbal and physical intervention.
04/20/95	One incident today of banging fists on table. Property destruction (throwing chairs). Floor restraint used.
04/21/95	Property destruction. Physical restraint.
04/25/95	Two incidents today. Bolted from workshop. Had to be restrained. Was taken to hospital by ambulance.

04/26/95	K.P. bolted from workshop and attempted to exit the building. Did not respond to verbal prompts. Had to be restrained.
05/03/95	Behavioral incident. Property destruction. Verbal intervention.
05/19/95	Property destruction. Pulled fire alarm. Use of quiet time room.
06/02/95	Slapping and biting self. Verbal intervention.
06/14/95	One incident of slapping head. Had to be restrained.
06/17-18/95	K.P. had two incidents in Petersburg, VA. Had to be restrained.
06/22/95	One incident of property destruction. Blanket wrap was used to calm him down.
06/23/95	Property destruction. Blanket wrap is used.
07/05/95	Inserted long bolt down throat. Verbal intervention was used.
07/07/95	Incident of property damage in the morning. Had to be restrained.
07/11/95	Running and hitting cars in parking lot. Restrained.

07/13/95   Incident of property destruction during lunch. Some face slapping. Had to be restrained.

07/24/95   Two incidents of property destruction. Had to be restrained.

08/08/95   Slapping self and property destruction. Restrained.

08/24/95   Banging windows with fists. Physically restrained. Running and beating on walls. Had to use physical restraint.

09/95   During the month of September there were five incidents of property damage. Verbal prompts and physical restraints were used.

10/04/95   Incident of property destruction. Restrained.

10/12/95   One incident of aggression and property destruction. Physical restraint.

10/13/95   Aggression toward another consumer. Physical restraint.

10/26/95   He was very agitated. One incident of aggressive behavior. Verbal intervention used.

10/27/95   One incident of running. Had to be restrained.

11/03/95	In hospital for monitoring. K.P. had two behavioral incidents in the hospital. Had to be restrained.
11/03/95	One incident of property destruction. Verbal intervention.
12/06/95	One incident of aggression and property destruction. Physical restraint.
12/15/95	Property destruction. Had to be restrained.
12/24/95	In Petersburg for Christmas. Had a behavioral outburst on Christmas Eve. Was taken to the hospital by ambulance because he was out of control for so long. He was given a shot of Thorazine.
12/26/95	Taken to the hospital again this morning. K.P. had another outburst. The doctor gave him Thorazine.
01/24/96	One incident of aggressive behavior and property destruction. Had to be restrained. I am praying for that MIRACLE.

APPENDIX A

Medical Records

EEG Reports

This 18-year-old boy has a long past history of
mental retardation and aggresive behavior. The
patient has had seizures in the past 5 years.
According to the patient's mother, in the past,
all seizures have been nocturnal. These are
grand mal in type. At times there is occasional
slobbering from the mouth and occasional
incontinence and always jerking. Evidently the
patient has had no seizures during the day at any
time.

In the past, the patient has been on
Phenobarbitol, Dilantin, and Tegretol. Evidently
all of these medications independently cause the
patient to be extremely aggressive and almost
uncontrollable. These have not been
discontinued. In April, 1986 all medications for
seizures were discontinued. However, 10 months
later, the patient had several further seizures.
In the past 1 year the patient has had 3 or 4
nocturnal generalized seizures.

At times, when the patient awakes in the morning,
the patient's mother can see that he is going to
"going to have a bad day". During these bad days
the patient has extreme aggressive behavior. In
the past he frequently has attached people. This
does not come on spontaneously as a seizure but
appears to be part of an aggressive personality
disorder. The patient understands poorly. He
does speak some. However, his degree of
retardation probably prohibits any type of
psychotherapy from being effective. When the
patient was a child, at age 8, Mellaril was given
for hyperactively, results unclear.

The patient's only present medication is
Depacote, 250 mg. t.i.d. given without ill effect
such as dizzines or drowsiness. A recnet
Depacote level according to the patient's mother
equal 48.   Other blood testing is pending.
Recently the patient has had difficulty sleeping
at night. Evidently sleeping pills and Valium
were used by Dr. ͡ ͜   with equivocal benefit.

NAME: **K.P.**

MR #:

DATE: 7/12/88

PROVIDER #526

GHA
Group Health Association
CLINICAL NOTES

PAGE 2 CONTINUED:

BRIEF EXAMINATION: Pupils are equal and reactive
to light. Visual fields are grossly full. There
is no nystagmus. Facial movement is symmetrical.
Gait is acceptable without ataxia.

IMPRESSION: Nocturnal generalized seizures not
completely controlled. Aggressive personality
disorder. Insomnia. Mental retardation.

RECOMMENDATIONS: The patient will increase
Depacote, 250 mg. tablets, and take 2 tablets
b.i.d. In 2 weeks the patient will go for a
morning Depacote level before dose is taken.
Then, call regarding this result. If the patient
awakes and "looks like he will have a bad day
with aggressiveness", the patient's mother will
give him Mellaril, 25 mg. t.i.d. on that
particular day (#30 with 3 refill). For sleep,
the patient will try Benadryl 25 mg. capsules, 2
q.h.s. If there are problems due to these
medications the patient's mother will call.
Otherwise return for follow up in 2 months.

M.D.

d. 7/12/88 t. 7/12/88 t. 7/18/88

NAME: K.P.

MR #:

DATE: 9/15/88

PROVIDER #526

GHA

Group Health Association

CLINICAL NOTES

In the past two months, the patient has had no
nocturnal or other seizure on Depakote 250 mg.
tablets, two p.o. b.i.d. without side effect
which he will continue (#100 with three refills).
Approximately once or twice per month, the
patient still has behavior problems during the
day. Also, there is moderate chronic insomnia.
The patient was given Mellaril. One tablet "put
him into a daze". Three tablets made him "too
hyper". There was some initial benefit by using
Benadryl but this wore off. In the past, the
patient has been on Valium. Haldol in the past
caused gynecomastia. Evidently the patient had
to be physically restrained on 6/29/88, 7/21/88,
8/18/88.

In addition to Depakote, the patient will begin
Clonopin 0.5 mg. tablets, one b.i.d. and two
q.h.s. (#30 with three refills). If there are
problems due to this medication, the patient's
mother will call.

A CBC, LDH, SGPT, and Depakote level will be
obtained.

The patient's mother has inquired about referral
to the NIH. There would be no reason to refer
the patient for seizures. However, the patient's
mother will inquire at the NIH regarding possible
entry into a program in the Psychiatry Department
for aggressive behavior and insomnia in a young
adult with moderate mental retardation. The
patient will return to Neurology in two months
for follow up.

M. D.

d. 9-15-88 r. 9-16-88 t. 9-20-88

55

NAME: K.P.

MR #:

DATE: 9/26/88

PROVIDER 526

3431

Group Health Association
CLINICAL NOTES

This patient's mother called today regarding complaints about K.P.' This patient has a past history of a seizure disorder. The patient's mother is aware and admits that this seizure problem is controlled by taking Depakote. This has been continued. In the past, when the patient took Dilantin, Tegretol, or Phenobarbital, he was "always going wild," according to the patient's mother. On Depakote the patient only "goes wild once a month." Evidently, this is tolerated by the patient's family and mother. However, despite the fact that he takes Depakote everyday, when the patient "goes wild" once per month, his mother still feels that this "might be the Depakote." This would be highly doubtful.

Recently, the patient's major problem has been difficulty sleeping. Frequently the patient does not sleep at all. The patient then becomes irritable and evidently bothers the family. Multiple medications have been tried for sleep, including Mellaril and Benadryl. Haldol has often been given in the past without benefit, and Valium also does not help. Recently, as a clinical trial, the patient was given Klonopin, which was given both for sleep and also because of its antiseizure effect. Evidently, because of Klonopin, the patient "even went more wild than usual." This required psychiatric intervention. The patient was admitted to a psychiatric hospital for two to three days at the end of last week and has now been discharged. He is now back in school. However, the patient's mother does not understand why I would give a medication of this type which would "just make him go psychotic." The patient's mother states this as an accusation, to some extent. However, later in the conversation the patient's mother did admit and state that "Everything is being done for K.P. at GHA that can be done." I advised the patient's mother that all medications are given by me in an effort, obviously, to help the patient. Obviously, medications of any type would not be given unless the patient's condition warranted giving such medication. In this case,

56

NAME: K.P.

MR # :

DATE: 9/26/88

PROVIDER 526

Page 2

medications have been given to help the patient
sleep because this is such a major problem. The
patient's mother is also made aware that any
specific medication may cause side effects, and
unfortunately the possible benefit cannot
absolutely be predicted before a medication is
taken. To some extent, the patient's mother
understands this. However, she also wonders how
K.P. would be "without any medicine." This could
always be considered. However, the patient's
mother is also advised that these medications are
all being given because of K.P.'s condition.

The patient's mother has asked me what I would do
if K.P. "was in my family." I advised the
patient's mother that all of my medical
recommendations are, to a great extent, "as if
the patient were a member of my family." I
advised the patient's mother that I would use
Benadryl, p.r.n. sleep, and I would continue
Depakote for seizures. The patient's mother is
advised that without medication for seizure, the
patient could go into status epilepticus. At
least for now, the patient's mother has agreed.

The patient's mother feels that at GHA we have
not referred the patient to NIH. However, I have
spoken to the patient's mother before and have
advised her that if the patient were accepted at
NIH under any type of protocol, either in
Neurology for seizures or in Psychiatry because
of behavior, a letter would be sent on this
patient's behalf for him to become involved. The
patient's mother, once again, is advised of this.
Certainly, I have no objections.

However, the patient's mother also feels that
"something has to be done." She feels that if he
is not accepted at the NIH, Group Health should
refer the patient "to Mexico or Africa or
anywhere that could help K.P. " From this
viewpoint the patient's mother, at times, is
quite irrational. *(As you can tell I was* G.H.
very frustrated and 8/30/91
willing to try any
type of medicine by now.)

57

GHA
Group Health Association
CLINICAL NOTES

Page 3

Hence, medications for now will be used as above.
Referral to NIH can be accomplished if K.P. would
be accepted under any protocol. A letter will be
provided. At this time, because of the patient's
mother being somewhat dissatisfied, the patient
will be referred to another neurologist at Group
Health to see "if he can think of anything better
to do."

M.D.

d:9/26/88 r:9/26/88 t:9/28/88

K.P.

CEEN WITHOUT MANCHART

CENTER: 1 2 (3) 4 5 6   Appt. Time /40
DEPT. 22   APPT. STATUS
1 ☒ Scheduled   PROVIDERS   Arr. Time / 30
2 ☐ Walk-in   1. 352
3 ☐ Write-in   2.   Appt. Length
8 ☐ Other   3.   ○15 ○20 ☒30
4/12/5   Date   Page   Min.

NUMBER	PROB. TITLE/DX		STATUS	Providers this Prob.
☐☐	SZ DISORDER ; BEHAVIOR		☐N ☐C ☐R	1 2 3

NUMBER	PROB. TITLE/DX	STATUS
☐☐	PROBLEM ; MILD (L) Hemiparess.	☐N ☐C ☐R

PROCEDURES & SERVS: ☐ Problem Work-up/Follow-up ☐ LP ☐ Suture Removal
☐ New Specialty Referral
☐ Tensilon Test

LAB ORDERS:
☐ CBC	☐ SMA-9	☐ IEP	☐ DPH
☐ Diff.	☐ Gluc. Tol 3 5	☐ Prot. Electrophoresis	☐ PB
☐ CSR (Sed. Rate)	☐ RPH	☐ T3, T4	☐ Mysoline
☐ B12	☐ Alk Phos, LDH, SGOT	☐ Urinalysis	☐ Depakene
☐ Folate		☐ Culture (Source):	☐ Other:

OTHER ORDERS:
☐ EKG	☐ Brain Scan	☐ NCV/EMG
☐ EEG	☐ CT Scan	☐ X-Ray
☐ OPG + Doppler	☐ ENG + Audiometry	☐ Evoked Response

PRESCRIP. (Rx) DILANTIN 200 - EVEN DAYS
300 - ODD DAYS.
☐ Free Sample
☐ Prescrip. Order
☐ Charge to Patient

DISPOSITION: ○ Return in ___ days ___ wks. ___ mos. ___ yrs./or ○ PRN for ○ 15 or ___ mins.
○ Tel. to/from Patient

REFERRED TO:

CLINICAL NOTE:
The patient returns for a follow-up visit for generalized seizures and a mild left congenital hemiparesis and mental retardation.

Since mother's last visit here, he was referred to Psychiatry because of increasingly violent behavior, both at home and at school. The mother indicates that the child was begun on Haldol by an outside psychiatrist. Unfortunately, this was only minimally helpful with behavior and did cause breast engorgement which was understandably distressing. Mother is currently seeking to have the child in a level-6 residential placement.

On physical examination today, the boy has mild end-point nystagmus on lateral gaze consistent with Dilantin administration. His coordination is good. The mild left hemiparesis with mild left hemiatrophy remains unchanged.

The patient's behavior is quite difficult to control. He acts according to the mother at the level of about a three-year-old boy. He is quite impulsive and has violent temper tantrums. In addition, he is quite tall and strong making this type of behavior quite difficult.

In my opinion, the only possible way that one could expect a change in K.P.'s behavior would be through an intensive behavioral modification program, preferably in a residential setting.

NEUROLOGY

Tel: Home
Work .
Birth Date 10-9-69
Age 15 yo   Sex ☒M ☐F
BP   Temp.
Head Circumference
General Appearance
Handedness R L
Mental States Exam   NL ___ ABN.
Cranial Nerves I
II Funduscopic
Visual Acuity O.D. O.S.
Visual Fields
III, IV, VI
V
VII
VIII
IX, X
XI
XII

☐ Continued

Form No. 2-22001   10/83

59

4/8/87   Neurology Note:

— K.P. has been seizure-free off tegretol, and behavior is usually fairly good. He had one major episode of behavioral problems, three weeks ago, but has been relatively good since + has not had screaming.

On exam he is echolalic, can follow a few simple directions - A quick glance at fundi does not reveal any abnormalities, no nystagmus. Tone, strength wnl, DTR's 1-2+ throughout, no tics, grimaces or abnormal movement noted. Gait nl, will not do tandem.

Plan - continue off anticonvulsants at present since has remained seizure free.

— MD.

EEG LABORATORY REPORT

Children's Hospital of the District of Columbia
2125 13th Street, N.W.
Washington 9, D. C.

		EEG	R-7357
NAME	K.P.	AGE	4 years
ADDRESS		PHONE	
	Rockville, Md. 20853		
		ROOM NO. OP-PVT 0182286/5

			cc:	Easter Seal Diagnostic
REFERRING DOCTOR	Dr.			Center of Mont. Co.
	CC:	Group Health Assn.		1000 Twinbrook Pkwy.
ADDRESS		2121 Pa. Ave., N.W.		Rockville, Md.
		Washington, D.C.		

REPORT   DATE: 15 November 1973

Medicated sleep tracing only was obtained and reveals
general activity of moderate to higher voltage mixed
theta and delta. In light sleep, well formed sleep
activity is seen bilaterally, usually synchronously.
On two occasions some low voltage spikes are seen coming
from either both central areas (page 057) or explicitly
from the left-central area (page 102). No sustained
seizure discharges, however, occur.

Sleep tracing is little changed from record of
12 July 1973.

SUMMARY: Abnormal EEG with occasional evidence of epileptogenic
activity, the significance of which must be interpreted
in light of the clinical presentation.

Doctor_____   _____
                                                M.D.

#670

GROUP HEALTH ASSOCIATION
2121 Pennsylvania Avenue, N.W.
Washington, D.C. 20037

EEG LABORATORY

EEG Report No. _127_   Date _4 Sept 75_

Address _____   _Rockville md 2085 3_

Age: _5 ½_ Diagnosis: _Hyperactivity, No Sz. Disorder and/or Mental retardation_

EEG FINDINGS AND INTERPRETATION:

The patient was presedated with 0.5 Gm. Chloral Hydrate prior to the test. The patient was in a sedated sleep throughout.

The tracing shows almost continuous Stage II through Stage IV range of sleep and is composed primarily of activities at 3-5 cycles per second with vertex sharp waves and poorly formed K-complexes and occasional sleep spindles at 12 cycles per second. There are rare medium amplitude spikes seen intermixed with this activity which may be artifactual, such as a cardiac manifestation coming through.

Hyperventilation and photostimulation were omitted.

Attempts at arousal were not successful electrographically.

IMPRESSION: The tracing is within normal limits in a sedated sleep state. It is recommended that a repeat tracing be obtained in three to six months and perhaps less sedation will be needed at that time.

GROUP HEALTH ASSOCIATION
ᴵ ᴵ 2621 Pennsylvania Avenue, N.W.
Washington, D.C. 20037

₹ ᵀ ∩ ᵀ ᴱ? 555

EEG LABORATORY

EEG Report No. __3288__   Date __4.22.81__

Rockville, Md. 20853

Addres.__

Age: __11 yro.__ Diagnosis: __R/o Seizures, Mental Retardation, Hyperactive. Re-evaluate__

EEG FINDINGS AND INTERPRETATION:

The EEG was recorded with the patient in the alert state. The
patient was uncooperative during the recording session and
frequent movement artefact obscures large portions of the record.
The portions of the record which can be interpreted showe well-
modulated 8-9 hertz alpha activity of low to moderate voltage
in the occipital derivations bilaterally symmetrical. Some low
voltage beta activity is present frontally and symmetrically.
No definite paroxysmal discharges are present.

Hyperventilation, and photic stimulation could not be done.

IMPRESSION: The portions of the EEG which can be interpreted
are within normal limits for the age of the patient.

63

APPENDIX B

Psychological Reports

Neuropsychological Report

RECEIVED MAR 8 1987 GM

Diagnostic and Professional Support Team
MONTGOMERY COUNTY PUBLIC SCHOOLS
Rockville, Maryland 20850

Report of Psychologist

Pupil's Name ___ K.P. _____ Student's ID # _____
Address   Rockville, MD 20853
School   National Children's Center _____

Date of Evaluation 87/02/24   Parent/Guardian ___ __ ____ ____
Date of Birth   69/09/02   Home Telephone __ _____
Age   17/05/22   Work Telephone _____

Sex   Male   Psychologist _____

Primary Language or Mode of Communication ___ English _____

ASSESSMENT TECHNIQUES USED

Beery VMI   Record Review
Classroom Observation   Stanford Binet
Developmental History   Teacher Conference
Draw-A-Person (DAP)   School Work Sample

REASON FOR REFERRAL

K.P.·- was referred for a psychological evaluation to determin
appropriate educational placement for the following year.

67

BACKGROUND

K.P. is presently in a residential program at National Children's
Center (NCC) in the District of Columbia. Prior to his enrollement at
NCC he had attended Longview Public Program in 1984. While in
Longview his behavior was violent and aggressive - eventually leading
to hospitalization. It was at this time he was recommended to NCC.
Participation in the current placement appears be beneficial to K.P.'s
developmental progress.

K.P. is verbal but usually waits for others to initiate communication.
He is able to express basic needs and wants by two or three word
utterances. Self- maintenance skills are advanced. History of Severe
Mental Retardation is recorded in addition to his aggression behavior
and seizure disorder.

Reports and interviews indicate that during the summer of 1986 K.P.
was treated for his seizures with Tegretol. His mother holds the
belief that this medication has had negative effects on K.P. Other
school personnel appear to share this opinion. K,P.'s physical health
is normal and a regular diet has been prescribed in the Center. Minor
medical notations show that the area between the 4th and 5th toe is
being treated with Tinactin cream for superficial fungi (athlete's
foot). Also, cocoa butter is continually applied to the
hyperpigmented area on left forearm.

Previous program reports state that K.P. is now in a self contained
Special Education class with 6 students, one certified teacher and two
teacher assistants. His program includes small group and
individualized instruction in social and emotional skills,
communication, pre-vocational abilities, and functional academics.
Behavior modification is used consistently throughout the day. He has
received Gym twice a week for 45 minute sessions; Life Skills four
times a week, 45 minute sessions for a three month period; and
individual Speech/Language therapy twice week, twenty minute sessions
for a three month period. K.P. is now on a Behavior Contract where
home visits are contingent on his good behavior, absence of aggression
or property damage. The home visit schedule is amended every other
weekend.

Parental regard, as well as NCC staff and personnel, toward current
placement appears to be favorable. Rapport is excellent between
family members and school. Homelife is highly positive and all are
extremely supportive of K.P.'s developmental needs socially,
emotionally, and intellectually. K.P., himself, to the extent that he
is able to perceive his own strengths and needs in a manner consistent
with his intellectual capacities , appears to be responding to his
placement and program in ways that could be interpreted as being more
positive than negative. This is observed through his decreased
agressive behaviors and increased productivity in schoolwork as the
weekend approaches for home visitation.

OBSERVATIONS

At the time of observation, K.P. was seated at an enclosed desk
working on an object manipulation task. Concentration was broken upon
seeing a new adult entering the room. K.P. found a timer which he
immediately threw over his back while saying, "There you go." Several
requests by the teacher's assistant to "pick it up" went unheeded by
K.P. . Time out was assigned by K.P., having to stand facing the wall.
K.P. appeared to accept this method of discipline quite well as he
picked up the clock after his time out period   (again with repeated
requests by the Teacher's assistant). As different adults entered the
room K.P. exhibited new behaviors such as getting up, walking around,
sitting at another student's desk, causing classroom disruptions,
emitting loud sounds and often requiring physical constraint by the
assistant.

Actual testing behavior consisted of K.P. breaking several pencils
into multiple pieces, short attention span, and K.P.'s inability to
stay in one place for more than a brief period. K.P. voiced his
verbal responses in a tone resembling a whisper. Testing was executed
with the aid of the assistant, (who physically restrained K.P. from
further disrupting the environment), until it was no longer possible
to continue. It is worthy of note, however, that in spite of the
distractions K.P. experienced he was able to follow certain
commissions from the examiner, execute tasks more easily when modeled,
and respond to verbal encouragement and praise.

TEST RESULTS

Stanford Binet - form LM Third Revision

Basal: II-0   Ceiling: III   Testing discontinued due to student's
                                 inability to test in a conventional
                                 manner.
Estimated Ratio IQ = 12 to 17   IQ derived from sum of testing,
                                 interviews with teacher and careful
                                 review of records.
Classification: Severe to Profound Mental Retardation - to be
                                 interpreted with caution.
DSM-III Code of measured intellectual functioning=319.0   UNSPECIFIED
                                 (IQ level is presumed to be below 70
                                 but individual is untestable.)

Beery Buktenica (VMI)

VMI Raw Score =   8 ; VMI Age Equivalent = 5-0

Draw-A-Person

Estimated standard score = <50
Estimated Mental Age Equivalent = <5-3
Estimated Quality Scale = <1
Estimated Percentile Rank = <1
Estimated general level of conceptual maturity = below the 1st
percentile rank for his age range.

Schoolwork Sample

K.P. was able to reproduce the lower case "r", trace his own first and
last name with dotted visual cues, spontaneously write the upper case
letters "K,H, and R" - letters contained in his names. K.P. also
perseveratively drew verticle rectangles containing a circle.
Visual/graphic execution-immature.

Vineland Adaptive Behavior Scales Classroom Edition - Revised

Score Summary

SUBDOMAIN	Standard Score	Band of Error 90% Confid.	Nat'l %ile	Stanine	Adaptive Level	Age Equiv.
Communication	25	± 7				
Daily Living Skills	43	± 5				
Socialization	57	± 6				
Adaptive Behavior Comp.	42	± 4	<.01	1	Low	4-0

Composite score is 4 Standard Deviations below Mean on an over-age
projection. (Scale is standardized to 12 years, 11 months, 30 days.)

DISCUSSION OF DATA

Results from the STanford Binet would indicate that K.P. is currently
functioning in the Severe to Profound range of Mental Retardation.
K.P. correctly completed the year II-0 level and one test in the year
II-6 level before testing was discontinued due to his inability to
test in a conventional manner. While this may be inconclusive it
would seem to further identify the true nature of his ability to
function in a structured situation requiring stratified degrees of
cognitive or motor processing. Testing indicates that K.P. is able to
recognize and manipulate forms, direct simple ideas combined with
memory span, comprehend simple speech, comprehend material, imitate
and experiment, attend and reason, meaningfully utilize two words but
not necessarily in a structurally correct manner, recognize familiar
objects by recall and verbal identification, and express himself
through special modes. He is also able to attach definitions to
concrete objects, focus on specific objects, exhibit purposive
response to verbal directions, demonstrate visual motor ability,
hand-eye coordination, and execute with modeling and by reproduction.

K.P.'s estimated level of general conceptual maturity as measured by
the DAP is below the 1%ile rank for category with a mental age
equivalent below 5 years.

K.P.'s ability for visual motor integration as measured by the Beery
VMI places him in the age equivalent range of 5 years-0 months.

Schoolwork sample reveals K.P.'s visual graphic ability to be at the
Pre-school level . He is able to write three out of ten letters
contained in his name.

Teacher's evaluations of .K.P.'s adaptive behavior skills
(Vineland-Revised) would indicate that his overall composite occurs 4
standard deviations below the standardized mean. This is an over-age
projection due to the nature of the researched population's age limit
-of 12-11-30. In this scale K.P.'s strength appears in Daily Living
Skills (Age Equiv. of 4-0). It is followed by Socialization (Age
Equiv. of 2-0) and finally Communication (Age Equiv. of 1-10. Total
composite places him lower than 0.1%, considered to be a LOW ADAPTIVE
LEVEL, and an Age Equiv. of 4 years -7 months.

SUMMARY

K.P. is a 17-6 year old male of substantial stature and strength.
Results from the Stanford Binet-LM indicate that he is currently
functioning in the Severe to Profound range of mental retardation.
This information should be used with caution. K.P.'s overall ability
and potential is not accurately reflected and this measurement might
not be reliable in the coming years. Relative cognitive strengths
appear to be evident in beginning language skills, simple reasoning,
and visual motor ability. K.P.'s level of Adaptive Behavior as
measured by the Vineland-R is found at the 4 year-7 months age range
with strengths in Gross Motor and Daily Living Skills, followed by
Socialization. K.P.'s weakest area is apparent in the Communication
subdomain (Age Equiv.- 1-10).

Major handicapping condition appears to be Severe to Profound Mental
Retardation complicated by language disorder and aggressive behaviors.

RECOMMENDATIONS

In view of the above the following is recommended:

1.   Progress, while it may not always be obvious, is evident in
      this small group/low student-teacher ratio class. Thus, current
      placement appears appropriate.

2.   Continued closely monitored 24 hour supervision.

3.   Utilization of primary reinforcers with gradual increase of
      limited well planned secondary reinforcers.

4.   Continued utilization of Behavior Management and Contract System.

                            School Psychologist
Copy to:
  DPST - Original
  Placement Unit

                                71

Diagnostic and Professional Support Team
Office for Special and Alternative Education
MONTGOMERY COUNTY PUBLIC SCHOOLS
Rockville, Maryland

Report of Psychologist

CONFIDENTIAL

Student's Name: K.P. Student's ID#:

Address: Rockville, Md. 20853

School: National Children's Center

Date of Evaluation: 2/2/89 Parent/Guardian:

Date of Birth: 10/6/69 Home Telephone:

Age: 19-3-26 Work Telephone:

Sex: Male Psychologist:

Primary Language or Mode of Communication: English

REASON FOR REFERRAL

K.P. was referred by the Central Placement Unit (CPU) of Montgomery County
public Schools (MCPS) to the school psychologist for a psychological
evaluation. The results of this assessment will be considered in the
determination of an appropriate educational program for K.P. next year.

ASSESSMENT TECHNIQUES

Stanford-Binet Intelligence Scale-Fourth Edition
AAMD Adaptive Behavior Scale (School Edition)
Classroom Observations
Teacher/Staff Conferences
Parent Conference
Record Review

BACKGROUND INFORMATION (Record Review, Teacher/Staff Conferences, Parent Conference)

K.P. is a nineteen year old male who, upon the referral of the CPU of MCPS has
been enrolled in the Level 5, non-public day program at the National
Children's Center (NCC) in Washington, D. C. since July, 1985. He was
enrolled in the residential program at NCC from July, 1985 until October, 1987
when he was discharged upon his mother's request. In November, 1987, the CPU
of MCPS accepted and formalized the request for K.P.'s discharge. K.P.
currently resides at the Great Oaks Center. This residential placement was
court ordered in October, 1988, because his behavior was no longer manageable
at home. K.P. has a previous diagnosis of moderate to severe mental

72

K.P.

DOB: 10/6/69

2

retardation, with a seizure disorder that is currently controlled by
medication. He also has a history of significant behavioral difficulties that
have been comprehensively documented in his confidential folder. Available
records indicate that K.P. has received Level 5 or Level 6 special education
services throughout his entire educational experience.

The results of K.P.'s most recent psychological evaluation (MCPS
2/24/87) were consistent with those of previous evaluations and suggest that
he continues to function within the severe to profound range of mental
retardation. Because his behavior significantly interfered with his
performance during this assessment, the examiner recommended that the results
be considered with caution.

Even though K.P. continues to have "good and bad" days in school, his teacher
and various staff members at NCC seem to feel that his "good" days are
becoming more frequent and that his behavior in the classroom has significantly improved. On "good" days,K.P. is very compliant, willing to work, and
capable of working up to 30 minutes on an independent assignment. On "bad"
days, K.P. is less compliant, exhibits destructive behavior (e.g., tearing
envelopes and bags), occasionally screams, and threatens to leave the
classroom without permission. He has not, however, exhibited any aggressive
behavior this year. Because he seems to thrive on negative attention during
"bad" times, his behavior is ignored whenever possible.K.P.'s ability to
perform pre-vocational/functional living skills appears to be a relative
strength. He has demonstrated the ability to collate papers, file
information, and stuff envelopes. He is also learning to write his first and
last name, count objects, recognize basic signs (e.g., "walk/don't walk,"
"men," "stop," etc.) and recite personal/identifying information upon
request. His ability to perform this latter task is hindered, however, by the
fact that his verbal/communication skills are significantly delayed. K.P.
seems to have adjusted very well to the transitions from Great Oak Center to
school and home on the weekends. His teacher also seems to feel that he would
be able to adjust and function very well in a sheltered workshop setting.
Because he continues to experience rare occasions of being out of control
(e.g., "bad days"), however, his teacher strongly recommends that future
placements for K.P.continue to include a plan for the management of his
behavior on "bad" days. Future educational plans for KlP. should also include
an emphasis on the further development of his functional living/vocational
skills.

K.P.'s mother   , seems to be pleased with K.P.'s overall educational
program and the amount of progress that he is making. She agrees that K.P.
has adjusted very well to the various transitions in his life (e.g., Great
Oaks Center to school and home on the weekends) and she has similarly noticed
an improvement in his behavior during weekend home visits. She also mentioned
that K.P. seems to look forward to and enjoy his weekly home visits. The
family similarly enjoys K.P.: home visits and would like to have him
living at home. They realize, however, that his behavioral outbursts are not
always predictable and consequently cannot always be managed at home. K.P.'s
mother expressed concern about K.P.'s future. While she agrees that he would
be a good candidate for a sheltered workshop, she does not seem to feel that
he is receiving adequate preparation for such a placement. Consequently, she
would like to see his current educational program place more attention on the

K.P.

DOB: 10/6/69

further development of his vocational/functional living skills. K.P.'s. mother also maintains her concern about his seizure medication and its side effects. She realizes that he must have the medication, however, and is pleased that his current medication seems to have minimal side effects compared to those of previous medications.

GENERAL OBSERVATIONS AND IMPRESSIONS (Classroom and Testing Behaviors)

K.P. was observed in his classroom while he was working on an independent task at his seat and while he was working on various daily living skills with his teacher. He seemed very distractible while he was working independently on a sorting task at his desk. He was constantly looking at the examiner, for example, and kept repeating the fact that his mother was coming to get him on the weekend. He similarly repeated all of the instructions that he heard the teacher give to other students in the classroom. He consistently followed simple instructions, however, and his attention was easily redirected with verbal prompting. Once he had finished the sorting task, he sat quietly at his desk, waiting for his turn to work with the teacher. K.P. was very cooperative while he worked on various functional living skills (e.g., what's your name?, your age?, your mom's name?, etc.) with his teacher. He consistently followed simple instructions and responded to simple questions. He was also very responsive to the positive feedback and attention that he received from his teacher. When the teacher had to leave the table unexpectedly to settle another student's behavior, K.P. sat patiently and his attention was easily refocused when the teacher returned. K.P.'s attention was also easily redirected whenever he seemed to be distracted by the behavior and voices of other students in the classroom.

K.P. was similarly very cooperative during the assessment. He willingly accompanied the examiner to the testing room and worked for approximately seventy-five minutes with two short breaks. He consistently followed simple instructions and willingly attempted all tasks. He seemed eager to please the examiner and was very responsive to praise and positive feedback. He frequently became involved in self-corrective behaviors and appeared to be instrinsically motivated to work on each task until completion. Although he occasionally seemed to be distracted by thoughts of his upcoming home visit or various noises in the nearby hallway, his attention was easily redirected. These observations are consistent with teacher and parental reports regarding K.P.'s behavior. Consequently, the results of this assessment are considered to be valid measures of his current level of functioning.

ASSESSMENT RESULTS

K.P.'s overall performance on the Stanford-Binet Intelligence Scale (Fourth Edition) fell within the upper limits of the severely mentally handicapped range of intellectual functioning and his level of performance was consistent across the Verbal Reasoning, Abstract/Visual Reasoning, Quantitative Reasoning, and Short-term Memory sections of this instrument (See test scores below).

Stanford Binet Intelligence Scale (Fourth Edition)

Standard Age Score SAS)

Verbal Reasoning	36**
Vocabulary	18
Comprehension	18
Absurdities	--
Verbal Relations	--
Abstract / Visual Reasoning	36**
Pattern Analysis	18
Copying	--
Matrices	--
Paper Folding and Cutting	--
Quantitative Reasoning	36**
Quantitative	18
Number Series	--
Equation Building	--
Short-Term Memory	36**
Bead Memory	18
Memory for Sentences	18
Memory for Digits	25
Memory for Objects	--

Test Composite

** For total and area SAS's, mean = 100, standard deviation = 16; for all
other scores, mean = 50, standard deviation = 8

-- Subtests omitted, or SAS off the table.

Within the verbal reasoning domain, K.P. received credit for his ability to
recognize and label pictures of common objects. His performance on this task
was similar to that of 2 year, 3 month-old children. K.P. similarly received
credit for his ability to identify various body parts (age equivalent = 3
years, 2 months). He did not, however, receive credit on any of the items
requiring him to provide verbal definitions for various words. His response
to these items was echolalic (i.e., he simply repeated the questions) and
seemed to be related to the fact that his verbal reasoning/expressive language
skills are severely delayed. His ability to verbalize his knowledge of common
behaviors and practices similarly seemed to be hindered by his verbal
reasoning/expressive language difficulties. K.P. also experienced difficulty
when he was asked to visually recognize and verbalize absurd relationships.
His lowered performance on this task seemed to be related to his high level of
visual distractibility. He continued to point randomly in spite of constant
verbal prompts for him to "look" at each picture. Within the quantitative
reasoning domain, K.P. received credit for his ability to count and match the
number of dots that were placed on the tops of three-dimensional blocks (age
equivalent = four years). His performance on this task seemed to reflect a
significant deficit in the area of acquired basic math reasoning skills.

Within the abstract/visual reasoning domain, K:P: experienced success when he
was asked to complete several form-boards within strict time limits. He was
less successful, however, when he was asked to match and reproduce geometric
designs through the manipulation of three-dimensional blocks, and did not
receive any credit on a task that required him to predict the pattern that
would be produced on a piece of paper that had been folded and cut. He
similarly experienced failure when he was asked to visually complete abstract
patterns by correctly selecting their missing parts. His lowered performance
on these tasks seemed to be related to visual-motor-integration difficulties
as well as visual attention difficulties. His overall performance on these
tasks was similar to that of children ranging in age from 3 years, 4 months to
3 years, 9 months. Within the short-term memory domain, K.P. received credit
for his ability to remember and repeat sentences and number sequences (age
equivalents = 2 years, 11 months and 5 years, 5 months, respectively). He
also received credit for his ability to remember and replicate patterns
involving beads of various shapes and colors (age equivalent = 3 years, 7
months). He did not receive credit, however, when he was shown a series of
pictures and asked to remember their order of presentation after they had been
placed among a new set of pictures. His lowered performance on this task
seemed to be related to the difficulty that he experiences when he is asked to
visually attend to details.

The AAMD Adaptive Behavior Scale (School Edition) was used to measure K.P.'s
current level of adaptive functioning and his teacher served as informant.
The scores are as follows:

AAMD Adaptive Behavior Scale (School Edition)

	Percentiles	
Part I	TMH	EMH
Independent Functioning	13-15	2-5
Physical Development	56	41
Economic Activity	55	3
Language Development	44	17
Numbers and Time	13	0
Prevocational Activity	38	45
Self-Direction	89	86
Responsibility	59	68
Socialization	20-25	14
Part II		
Aggressiveness	0	5
Antisocial vs. Social Behavior	25	34
Rebelliousness	15	16
Trustworthiness	--	--
Withdrawal vs. Involvement	45	50
Mannerisms	--	--
Interpersonal Manners	20	6
Acceptability of Vocal Habits	11	3
Acceptability of Habits	22	16
Activity Level	--	--
Symptomatic Behavior	33	33
Use of Medications	13	0

K.P.
DOB: 10/6/69

These percentile scores are comparing K·P· to students whose developmental
levels range from 16 years, 3 months to 17 years, 2 months (as these age
levels represent the upper limits of this scale) and who have been placed in
classrooms for the Trainable Mentally Handicapped (TMH) and the Educable
Mentally Handicapped (EMH), respectively. According to his teachers' report,
K.P.'s current level of adaptive functioning is consistent with his current
level of intellectual functioning in the areas of cognitive development,
socialization, prevocational activity, and independent functioning. That is,
his level of adaptive behavior in these areas falls significantly below that
of children in TMH and EMH classrooms. In the areas of self-direction and
responsibility, however, K.P. compares quite favorably to students in both the
TMH and EMH classrooms. His behavior would also be acceptable in classrooms
for TMH or EMH students.

SUMMARY AND RECOMMENDATIONS

K.P. is a nineteen year old male who has been enrolled in the Level 5,
non-public day program at NCC since July 1985. He has a previous diagnosis of
moderate to severe mental retardation, with a seizure disorder that is
currently controlled by medication. He also has a history of significant
behavioral difficulties that significantly interfere with his ability to learn
and function in a classroom setting. The results of this assessment are
consistent with those of previous attempts to measure K.P.'s cognitive and
adaptive abilities, and suggest that he continues to function within the
moderate to severe range of mental retardation.

Because his needs continue to be multiple and extensive in nature, it is
recommended that K.P. continue to receive Level 5 special educational services
in school. It is recommended that his program continue to be highly
structured, with a low teacher/student ratio. It is also recommended that his
program continue to emphasize the further development of his daily
living/vocational skills, so that he will be adequately prepared should the
possibility of a sheltered-workshop position be considered for him in the
future. K.P.'s parents, teachers, and various staff members at NCC should be
commended for their combined interests and involvement in his educational
planning and overall well-being. They should also be encouraged to continue
their involvement so as to ensure the continuation of an appropriate education
for K.P.

School Psychologist

4/4/89

Copy to
DPST - original
Central Placement Unit
Parent

Psychological Services
Specializing in Neuropsychology

CONFIDENTIAL

Neuropsychological Evaluation:

Re: K.P.
Age: 24 years (dob 10/06/69)
Date of Evaluation: 9/22/94 Baltimore Office
Reason for Evaluation: Explosive Behavior
Referred by: MedSource Community
                              Services, Inc.

Tests Administered: Aphasic and Perceptual Screening
                              Finger Tapping
                              Grip Strength
                              Digit Symbol
                              Projective Drawings

                              Interview with Staff
                              Review of Records

Relevant History and Clinical Observations:

   K.P.   is a 24 year old single male who presents
with overt signs of Retardation and communication problems.
Upon introduction, he was immediately tense, rolling his eyes
and pulling toward staff away from the examiner. After
gentle assurance and with the help of staff he entered the
examing room alone and was cooperative for more than two hours.

   He is being evaluated because of adjustment problems at
his group home residence and at his workshop assignment. He
sometimes becomes agitated and runs uncontrollably, sometimes
to a nearby residence, and trys to throw or break things. He
He also has been observed trying to hurt himself such as
slapping and biting. He has torn off his clothes and has tried
to bite others. Although these behaviors have been present for
sometime, the last two or three months show more frequency and
deterioration.

   He was born with paranatal problems including seizures.
Things became worse after age 7 and again at age 13 years. He
is under medical care and being medicated with Depakote. Staff
report he is sleeping and eating well. With some assistance
K.P. can care for himself.

   He likes to listen to music and at times can be pleasant.
He does have a sense of self but is non-conversational. He
loves kickball, individual attention but can get over excited
and is very sensitive to temperature, hot/and or cold.

Test Results:

Aphasic and Perceptual Screening: He recognizes and reproduces
shapes but cannot name them. He copies shapes with his left
hand and responds best when a model is demonstrated vs. verbal
or picture presentation. He prints his name but shows spontaneous letter reversals. He is very quick, almost impulsive

78

CONFIDENTIAL

when demonstration is provided but does not initiate and
remains immoble when given oral requests. Some requests
were responded to only after significant delay. He was
unable to read or write and yet was able to understand verbal
instructions even when he could not respond motorically. He
enjoyed praise and was often echolalic, " K.P. did good".

Interpretive Impression: Some preservation of Posterior
Cortical Function, Right Brain but marked problems Subcortical
and Left Brain.

Finger Tapping: Able to tap 5 and up to 35 with help (50 is
expected). Right hand performance was much worse with erratic
hand jerking and twisting body movements especially in the
neck area.

Interpretive Impression: Subcortical and Left Brain Dysfunction.

Grip Strength: Right hand 21 kg, left hand 31 kg (40-50 kg
expected)

Interpertive Impression: Left Brain Frontal-Temporal Lobe
Dysfunction.

Digit Symbol: Unable to follow instructions but copied the
numbers over the existing numbers.

Interpretive Impression: Some preservation of Right Brain but
Left Brain Dysfunction.

Projective Drawings: Person and Tree were recognizable but the
House lacked outside boundaries. Details were suprisingly
very good but poorly integrated.

Interpretive Impression: Subcortical and Cortical (probably
Frontal-Temporal lobe) synthesis Dysfunction but Brain Areas
working in isolation.

Other Observations: He tends to work with the left hand leading
but will use right hand on right side and left hand on left
side with little is defensive to midline crossover. He chunks
his food with rapid eating and drinking. Although hand strength
is adequate, touch and hand shake is very light and with poor
muscle tone. Eye movements are poor, reluctant and erratic.
He is very sensitive to auditory signals and physical approach.

Interpretive Impression: Subcortical Dysfunction.

Summary and Clinical Impression:

K.P. is seen as having Subcortical and Left Hemis-
phere (Frontal-Temporal) Encephalopathy. Essentially, this
results in a Dysarousal, and Dysregulation condition.

CONFIDENTIAL

Generally, he is seen as Underaroused causing inattention, easy distractibility, and confused about input or expectations. Sometimes, certain signals, i.e. Auditory, and Spatial are hyperintense because of lack of natural balance from other stimulation, therefore, he responds defensively, echolalic, perseveration, and impulsively.

His condition is seen as intermittant and cyclical. This will complicate things because at times he seems able to handle expectations, i.e. Workshop, but at other times can have very dramatic change.

His Encephalopathy is consistent with Autism, Complex and Simple Partial Subclinical Seizures, and Attention Deficit Disorder.

He is seen as having much more potential than he is now able to show.

Recommendations and Suggestions:

1). Medical review for Dysarousal Syndrome: Medication and EEG.

2). Simplify his expectations at home/workshop until he improves.

3). Immediately initiate Neurobehavioral Intervention Activities such as sports, music, dance/movement and other gross motor tasks such as rocking, walking, washing/polishing large objects (car). Occupational Therapy can be very helpful.

4). Immediately instruct in "stop breath" and slow breath exhale to be practiced no less than 3 times per day. After learned, then it can be used for Behavioral Management.

5). Use "wrap-up" around self i.e. foam blanket around body to prevent escalation of agitation and to promote calming.

6). Ongoing Neuropsychological Consultation weekly to monitor above recommendations and to further instruct staff regarding special exercises:

A) Stencil training
B) Blind box training
C) Brain talk
D) Fine motor training as in use of clay

7). Immediate use of Neurofeedback. SMR training as soon as it becomes available in the community.

Thank you for allowing me to see K.P..

Clinical and Consulting Neuropsychologist

APPENDIX C

Individualized Education Program

NATIONAL CHILDREN'S CENTER, INC.

INDIVIDUALIZED EDUCATION PROGRAM

1. Identifying Information

   Name of Student __K.P.__   Birthdate __10/6/69__   Age __20__

   School __National Children's Center__   Teacher _____

   Name of Parent/Guardian _____   Phone Number _____

   Address _____ Rockville, MD 20853 _____

2. Date of Annual IEP Meeting __3/29/90__ Date of Interim Meeting __Projected: 11/90__

3. Period of Plan: From __5/90__ to __12/90__ Annual Review Date: _____

4. Special Notations

   a. Health Status, Visual and Hearing Acuity __Seizure disorder treated with Depakote__
      __500mg in AM and 250mg in PM. Unable to screen vision 10/89. Passed hearing__
      __screening 9/89. Needs a current dental screening.__

   b. Observed Learning Style __All modalities__

   c. Other __Reinforcers: Praise, self-satisfaction, showing completed work to mother,__
      __time and space alone, money.__

5. Parent Notification (Document efforts to involve parents):

Date(s)	Method of Contact	Resulting Action
2/22/90	Letter to mother	Scheduled IEP
3/21/90	Reminder letter to mother	Confirm IEP
3/28/90	Telephone call to mother	Confirm IEP
3/29/90	IEP meeting hold	Mother attended

6. Proposed Instructional Services (include suggested ratios, suggestions for programming, etc.): Highly structured, self-contained classroom with teacher:student ratio of 1:3; Classroom language stimulation for a minimum of 30 minutes per month; Monthly consultation between speech/language pathologist and teacher; Bi-weekly consultation between psychologist and teacher.

7. Hours per week in regular education: __0__ ; in physical education: __1½__

8. Transportation: __Montgomery County Public Schools__

83

Name of Student ___K.P.___   Birthdate ___October 6, 1969___

10. TESTING INFORMATION

Test Name	Date Administered	Test Administrator	Score and Interpretation
Zimmerman et. al. Preschool Language Scale	4/4/90 & 4/5/90	MS, CLC-SLP Speech/Lang. Path.	Auditory Comprehension Age = 3 years, 1½ months (point score = 17) Expressive Language Age = 2 years, 10½ months (point score = 15) Language Age = 3 years, 0 months
Peabody Picture Vocabulary Test-Revised (Form M)	5/30/89		Raw Score = 30 Age Equivalent = 3 years, 3 months
Gardner Expressive One-Word Picture Vocabulary Test	4/4/89		Raw Score = 21 Age Equivalent = 2 years, 3 months
Boehm Test of Basic Concepts - Preschool Version	5/30/89 & 5/31/89		Total Correct = 26 of 52 Percentage = 50%
Goldman-Fristoe Test of Articulation	5/31/89		ERRORS Initial - d/θ, b/v, x/z Medial - ts/tʃ, ʃ/l, -/θ, b/v, d/ʒ Final - x/tʃ, -/r, s/dʒ, f/θ, x/s, -/z Blends - b/bl, kw/kl, pw/pl sw/skw
Oral-Peripheral Examination	5/30/89		Within normal limits

Birthdate <u>10</u>/<u>06</u>/<u>70</u>

TESTING INFORMATION

BRIGANCE INVENTORY: Date Administered <u>03</u>/<u>30</u>/<u>90</u>

Administered by Classroom Teacher

Gross Motor Skills
Range: <u>4-6 to 7-0</u>

Fine Motor Skills
Range: <u>3-8 to 7-0</u>

Self-Help Skills
Range: <u>3-0 to 7-0</u>

Speech and Language
Skills
Range: <u>2-0 to 4-4</u>

General Knowledge and
Comprehension
Range: <u>3-0 to 7-0</u>

Readiness Skills
Range: <u>2-8 to 7-0</u>

Basic Reading Skills
Range: <u><5-3</u>

Manuscript Writing Skills
Range: <u><5-6 to 6-3</u>

Math Skills
Range: <u>4-0 to 6-0</u>

<u>Possible Ranges on Subtests</u>

Gross Motor Skills:	1-0 to 7-0
Fine Motor Skills:	0-7 to 7-0
Self Help Skills:	0-0 to 7-0
Speech and Language Skills:	0-6 to 7-0
General Knowledge and Comprehension:	1-6 to 7-0
Readiness Skills:	1-6 to 7-0
Basic Reading Skills:	5-3 to 7-0
Manuscript Writing Skills:	5-3 to 7-0
Math Skills:	1-6 to 7-0

85

Name of Student ___K.P.___ Birthdate ___October 6, 1969___

11. Present Level of Educational Functioning:

Prevocational Skills: K.P. has achieved numerous goals in preparation for future employment. This is definitely the area in which K.P.'s talents are evident. He has excellent work habits. He can consistently work for an hour independently, maintaining a high standard of productivity and quality. He works well both alone and on a production line, even when faced with potential distracting behaviors of other students. K.P. has successfuly performed numerous jobs in a variety of settings. First, he has participated in a duplicating service, xeroxing with assistance, collating, criss-crossing, stapling and paper clipping, with minimal assistance. He has successfully performed all the steps for completing advertisement mailings for an insurance company, involving folding, stamping, sealing, and placing on address labels. Another job at school has been to stock three xerox rooms with paper. Additionally, he can independently do the third floor trash collection. One of his favorite vocational jobs has been folding pizza boxes at school for Domino's. He also has delivered hundreds of boxes, on a weekly basis, to Domino's, via school bus. Another community job he has successfully performed is delivering coat hangers to Casual Corner dress shops. Finally, K.P. has done well performing many in-class jobs such as sweeping the carpet and washing desk tops.

Communication: K.P.'s most recent speech and language evaluation was conduced in April and May 1989; the results indicated that he was functioning approximately at the three year language level, with a severe language disorder as well as a profound delay. His spontaneous use of language has increased over the past two years. He has made good progress in his ability to request items and ask about/comment on things that puzzle or upset him. The majority of the utterances that he uses are rote and are between three to six words in length. He also uses a great deal of echolalia, both immediate and delayed. Echolalia often serves a purpose for K.P.; that is, he repeats things when he is unsure of them as a sort of "mental rehearsal" or to reassure himself that everything is as it is supposed to be. Once he has repeated an utterance, he will then perseverate on it. Ignoring K.P. does not usually end his perseverations. A more successful method of dealing with him is to either repeat the sentence that he is perseverating on back to him or to respond to it in some way. In class and language therapy this year, K.P. has learned to follow prepositional commands involving the preposition under. He is currently working on in front of and in back of. He is able to select the correct picture when given a functional description (i.e., "What do you action with?") for ten common items. He continues to work on giving the functions of those same ten items when asked. He can now answer yes/no questions meaningfully in regard to his needs and wants, but not those questions dealing with object identities (i.e., "Is this a cup?") or acivities in his environment. K.P. will be discharged from individual therapy this year so that he may concentrate on his prevocational and vocational skills. However, consultative and language stimulation services will still be provided, focusing on maintaining existing skills, answering functional questions, increasing his vocabulary for vocational concepts, and increasing his ability to request more materials, as needed. He passed a hearing screening in September 1989.

Social Emotional: K.P. has maintained a near zero rate for his previous maladaptive behaviors for almost two years. He has not demonstrated any property destruction, inappropriate voiding, or screaming.

86

Name of Student _____ K.P. _____ Birthdate ___ October 6, 1959 ___

11. Present Level of Educational Functioning:

K.P. has shown, on a consistent basis, that he has matured emotionally and
socially. He is demonstrating much better control of his behavior. He is
consistently compliant, on-task, in his seat, and attending well. K.P. enjoys being with others, but also likes his solitude time. He likes to talk
with others especially staff, but also chooses to take leisure time alone to
play table games such as Connect Four. He will play with peers, especially
if staff supervised. K.P.'s reinforcers are mainly the enjoyment, self-
satisfaction and praise from a job well done. He also likes getting paid
and going to the school store.

Academic/Cognitive: K.P. has many pre-academic skills. These skills include
matching and sorting shapes and colors, identifying the letters of his first
name, and rote counting 1-10. In reading, K.P. can receptively and expres-
sively identify the symbols for men and stop. In writing, he can print his
first name from memory, and can print his last name while looking at a model.
In math, he can sort coins and sometimes identify penny and quarter. He can
count out 1 and 2 functional objects. He understands that money is needed
to purchase items. Finally, he can give personal identification information
including his full name, his mother's name,   his school, and
his mother's town and state, and his former place of residence at Great Oaks.

Self-Help: K.P. can perform most self-help skills. He is very neat in
appearance and in his self-help skills. He independently performs all
toileting, eating and dressing skills. In grooming, he independently
brushes his teeth, washes and dries his hands, and with prompting, can
brush his hair. K.P. has always been good about cleaning up after himself.

Motor/Perceptual: In gross motor skills, K.P. has done very well. He is
especially excellent in swimming and tumbling. He is also on the NCC
Special Olympic roller skating team, and will be on the swim team too. He
performs all of his gross motor skills in a mature fashion. In fine motor
skills, K.P. can print his first name from memory. He can draw circles,
squares, and a person. He does extremely well in manipulating small objects and constructing things, e.g., folding pizza boxes and assembling
electrical fittings. He can use scissors to cut out simple shapes.

Community-Based Skills: K.P. has learned many community-based skills this
year in the areas of traveling, shopping, and eating in restaurants. In
using the Metro subway, he can independently perform all steps in using his
fare card to enter and exit the subway. He can perform over half the steps
for waiting and riding the subway independently, and the rest with minimal
verbal prompts. When taking the Metro bus, he can do so with minimal verbal prompting. In shopping, K.P. can now perform all the steps for pur-
chasing a item with minimal verbal prompts. At fast food restaurants, with
verbal prompts, he can give his order and pay for it. He also has fine
table manners in public and cleans up after himself.

Name of Student __K.P.__

Birthdate __October 6, 1969__

12. Prioritized Annual Goals	Short-Term Objectives* (*Include Eval. Procedures & Criteria)	Special Education Resources/Services (Cite Curriculum)	Projected Dates
I. Prevocational Skills A. K.P. will improve his work behaviors.	1. Given a workshop simulated setting and a known task, K.P. will work alone for a two hour session, with a 10 minute break, with minimal verbal prompts, on 4 out of 5 days, for one month.	Classroom Teachers	5/90 - 12/90
	2. Given a simulated workshop setting and a known task, K.P. will work cooperatively with one or more students, for a two hour session, with a ten minute break, with minimal verbal prompts, on 4 out of 5 days, for one month.	Classroom Teachers	5/90 - 12/90
	3. Given a variety of known tasks, K.P. will independently gather the materials for the task, set up the task, ask for materials when he runs out, and put the materials away when completed, on 4 out of 5 trials, for 1 month.	Classroom Teachers	5/90 - 12/90
B. K.P. will improve his prevocational skills.	K.P. will independently perform a variety of mail service tasks: (a) criss-crossing collated reports; (b) using the business letter fold, (c) placing on stamps, with 80% accuracy, for 3 consecutive days.	Classroom Teachers DC-CBC Obj. SE-MS-C05	5/90 - 12/90
C. K.P. will perform work tasks in normalized settings.	Given a variety of jobs (in-school and community-based) with minimal supervision, will complete his job twice a week, with 80% accuracy, for 3 consecutive weeks.	Classroom Teachers	5/90 - 12/90
D. K.P. will improve his work adjustment skills.	Given a variety of work settings, with normal environmental distractors,K.P. will remain on task, with no more than 1 verbal prompt, for 3 consecutive days. Evaluation Method: As measured by formal and informal testing.	Classroom Teachers	5/90 - 12/90

88

Name of Student _____ K.P. _____   Birthdate   October 6, 1969

Prioritized Annual Goals	Short-Term Objectives* (*Include Eval. Procedures & Criteria)	Special Education Resources/Services (Cite Curriculum)	Projected Dates
II. Communication A. K.P. will improve his vocational language skills.	1. Given a specified vocational task and only part of the necessary materials (i.e., 50 letters to insert and only 35 envelopes), will (a) obtain a staff member's attention, (b) request the item necessary to finish, for 3 different tasks, on 4 of 5 consecutive days.	Classroom Teacher Monthly consultation between classroom teachers and speech/language pathologist	5/90 - 12/90
	2. Given object stimuli, K.P. will identify the concepts top and bottom, as related to vocational commands (i.e., "Put the paper on top of the pile. Put the label on the bottom of the page.") (a) when presented separately (b) when presented in random order, with 80% accuracy, for 3 consecutive days.	Same as above	(a) 5/90 - 9/90 (b)10/90 - 12/90
B. K.P. will improve his ability to answer questions.	Given situational stimuli, K.P. will (a) maintain his ability to answer yes/no questions regarding wants and needs, (b) answer yes/no questions regarding activities that he is engaged in (i.e., "Are you finished working?"), with 80% accuarcy for 3 of 4 consecutive days. Evaluation Method: As measured by formal and informal testing.	Same as above	(a) 5/90 - 12/90 (b 5/90 12/90
III. Social/Emotional A. K.P. will improve his social interaction skills.	1. K.P. will initiate a leisure-time activity with a peer on 2/4 occasions per week, for one month.	Classroom Teachers Biweekly consultation between psychologist and teachers	5/90 - 12/90
	2.K.P. will engage in a leisure time activity with a peer for 15 minutes, on 3/4 occasions per week, for 1 month.	Same as above	5/90 - 12/90

89

Name of Student _____ K.P. _____

Birthdate October 6, 1989

Prioritized Annual Goals	Short-Term Objectives* ("Include Eval. Procedures & Criteria)	Special Education Resources/Services (Cite Curriculum)	Projected Dates
12. B. K.P. will increase his assertiveness.	When touched or handled inappropriately by a peer,K.P. will say "stop" and turn away from that person, 75% of the time, for 2 months. Evaluation Method: As measured by formal and informal testing.	Classroom Teachers Biweekly consultation between psychologist and teacehrs	5/90 - 12/90
IV. Functional Academics A. K.P. will improve his ability to give personal data, when needed.	1. When asked any personal identification information, K.P. will independently present a personal ID kept in his wallet, 80% of the time, for one month.	Classroom Teachers	5/90 - 12/90
	2. When asked, K.P. will correctly give the following information: (a) his telephone number, (b) his address, with 80% accuracy for 3 consecutive days.	Classroom Teachers	5/90 - 12/90
B. K.P. will acquire survival reading skills.	Given 5 boxes and 5 cans of food items, K.P. will receptively and expressively identify each, with 80% accuracy, for 3 consecutive days.	Classroom Teachers	5/90 - 12/90
C. K.P. will acquire functional math skills.	When asked about the cost of 5 items (1¢ and 50¢ items), K.P. will match the coins (one penny and 2 quarters), with the correct items with 80% accuracy, on 2 consecutive days. Evaluation Method: As measured by formal and informal testing.	Classroom Teachers LEAPS: Functional Arithmetic Obj II	5/90 - 12/90
V. Self-Help K.P. will increase his grooming skills.	1. Following the steps of a task analysis, K.P. will independently (a) brush and (b) comb his hair correctly, with 80% accuracy for 5 consecutive days.	Classroom Teachers LEAPS: Grooming Obj. II-B	5/90 - 12/90

90

Birthdate _____ October 6, 1969 _____

Prioritized Annual Goals	Short-Term Objectives* (*Include Eval. Procedures & Criteria)	Special Education Resources/Services (Cite Curriculum)	Projected Dates
12.	2. With close supervision, K.P. will clip his fingernails, once a week, for one month. Evaluation Method: As measured by formal and informal testing.	Classroom Teachers LEAPS: Grooming Obj. II-C	5/90 - 12/90
VI. Community-Based Skills A. K.P. will develop shopping skills.	K.P. will independently purchase an item from a store, for 3 consecutive days.	Classroom Teachers	5/90 - 12/90
B. K.P. will develop traveling skills.	K.P. will independently wait appropriately for a subway car or bus and appropriately enter, ride, and exit, for 3 consecutive days.	Classroom Teachers LEAPS: Mobility Training Objs. V & VI	5/90 - 12/90
C. K.P. will develop restaurant skills.	K.P. will independently give his order in a restaurant, for 3 consecutive days. Evaluation Method: As measured by formal and informal testing.	Classroom Teachers	5/90 - 12/90
VII. Independent Living Skills K.P. will improve his independent living skills.	1.K.P. will independently operate the washer with 85% accuracy, during three consecutive trials.	NCC Task Analysis Life Skills Instructor Classroom Teachers	1990 - 91 Life Skills
	2.K.P. will independently iron a dress shirt, with 85% accuracy, during three consecutive trials.	Same as above	1990 - 91 Life Skills

Name of Student ___ K.P. ___

Birthdate ___ October 6, 1969 ___

12. Prioritized Annual Goals	Short-Term Objectives* (*Include Eval. Procedures & Criteria)	Special Education Resources/Services (Cite Curriculum)	Projected Dates
	3. K.P. will independently fold school laundry, with 85% accuracy, during three consecutive trials. Evaluation Method: As measured by formal and informal testing.	NCC Task Analysis Life Skills Instructor Classroom Teachers	1990 - 91 Life Skills

APPENDIX D

Individual Habilitation Plan

VOCATIONAL STRENGTHS / INTERESTS / NEEDS

This list should be combined with the residential list (as applicable). Prioritized needs are to be ranked by the entire team.

STRENGTHS & COMPETENCIES	INTERESTS / PREFERENCES
K.P. is in good overall health and has good gross motor skills. He can write his own name and print some numbers. K.P is independent in most ADL skills and can communicate his wants and needs.He is friendly, polite and likes to greet people. K.P can work for uo to two hours on a familiar task with minimal contact from his supervisor. He can learn new tasks when modeled by his supervisor.	K.P. enjoys sports requiring gross motor skills. He enjoys listening to and playing music, drawing and watching television. K.P. regularly works recycling negatives, though he will engage in work which requires gross motor activity. He prefers a quiet atmosphere and is generally a lofer at work. He has lately begun initiating interaction with staff and peers, especially in relation to work activities.

NEEDS & RECOMMENDATIONS FOR GOALS / SERVICES

Long Range Plan: Decrease incidents of disruptive behavior through development of mid-brain integration techniques. Review status in one year to determine direction for vocational training/development.

Prioritized Needs	Goals / Services	Responsible
(1) Develop independence in mid-brain integration techniques to reduce incidents of disruptive behavior.	Goal 95.1 - Learn/participate in two mid-brain integration excersises	VSI
(2) Staff training in Management of Disruptive Behavior to ensure the safety of .K.P and others during episodes of violent behavior.	Service - Two trained staff available at all times in the event physical restraint is needed.	VSI
(3) Maintain communication between providers and family to provide consistent training and fedback.	Service - Daily communication log between day and residential programs and frequent communication with K.P. mother.	VOI Medsource
(4) Increase expressive communication outlets to facilitate socialization.	Service - Weekly group movement therapy	ASG
(5) Encourage independent interactions with staff and peers	Service - Frequent reinforcement of social interaction	VSI

95

NAME: K.P.   IHP DATE: 2/10/95

VSI - IHP GOAL / OBJECTIVES # 1 OF 1

GOAL: (#95.1)* K.P.will participate in and learn mid-brain integration excercises to calm himself
      when agitated.

TARGET[ACTUAL] DATE: IMPLEMENTATION   [3/1/95]   COMPLETION   [2/96]

OBJECTIVE: (#95.1 a) K.P will participate in and learn stop breath excercises for 30 consecutive
      trials days.

TARGET[ACTUAL] DATE: IMPLEMENTATION   [3/1/95]   COMPLETION   [8/95]

OBJECTIVE: (#95.1.b) K.P will participate in and learn brain talk excercises 3 times weekly for six
      consecutive trials months.

TARGET[ACTUAL] DATE: IMPLEMENTATION   [9/95]   COMPLETION   [2/96]

OBJECTIVE: (# .c)

TARGET[ACTUAL] DATE: IMPLEMENTATION   [   ]   COMPLETION   [   ]

OBJECTIVE: (# .d)

RESPONSIBLE: COORDINATOR / QDDP: STAFF:

COMMENTS / REVISIONS:

* NUMBER GOALS ACCORDING TO IHP YEAR AND PRIORITY (i.e., 96.1 & 95.2)

Suggestions for K.P.'s problem
including alternative healing
and medication, etc. should be
directed to:

Eleanor Hinton
P.O. Box 1954
Petersburg, VA 23805

About the Author

Eleanor Hinton is an educator and school guidance counselor who has been employed at the elementary, middle and high school levels, as well as in adult educational settings. She provides counseling services to children, adolescents, their parents and teachers in the mainstream school setting. In addition, Ms. Hinton counsels the special needs population, including the physically handicapped, mentally disabled, juvenile delinquents and children with emotional problems. She has attended and participated in many seminars on the behavior of children, adolescents and adults.

Ms. Hinton holds a Master's Degree and has earned sixty additional graduate credits in Guidance and Counseling.

The author is the recipient of many professional awards in Guidance and Counseling and is known for her sense of humor and down-to-earth style.

To order additional copies of **Waiting for a Miracle**, complete the information below.

Ship to: (please print)

Name _____

Address _____

City, State, Zip _____

Day phone _____

___ copies of *Waiting for a Miracle* @ $10.99 each $_____

Postage and handling @ $2.50 per book $_____

Virginia residents add 4.5% tax $_____

Total amount enclosed $_____

Make checks payable to *Nosam Enterprise*

Send to: **Waiting for a Miracle**
P.O. Box 1954 • Petersburg, Virginia 23805

To order additional copies of **Waiting for a Miracle**, complete the information below.

Ship to: (please print)

Name _____

Address _____

City, State, Zip _____

Day phone _____

___ copies of *Waiting for a Miracle* @ $10.99 each $_____

Postage and handling @ $2.50 per book $_____

Virginia residents add 4.5% tax $_____

Total amount enclosed $_____

Make checks payable to *Nosam Enterprise*

Send to: **Waiting for a Miracle**
P.O. Box 1954 • Petersburg, Virginia 23805